Life After Death

Life After Death

New and future titles in the series include:

Alien Abductions

Angels

Atlantis

The Bermuda Triangle

The Curse of King Tut

Dragons

Dreams

ESP

The Extinction of the Dinosaurs

Extraterrestrial Life

Fairies

Fortune-Telling

Ghosts

Haunted Houses

Jack the Ripper

The Kennedy Assassination

King Arthur

The Loch Ness Monster

Pyramids

Stonehenge

UFOs

Unicorns

Vampires

Witches

The Mystery Library

Life After Death

Nancy Hoffman

LUCENT
BOOKS ®

THOMSON

™

GALE

San Diego • Detroit • New York • San Francisco • Cleveland • New Haven, Conn. • Waterville, Maine • London • Munich

On Cover: *The Inscription over the Gate*, William Blake (1757–1827).

LIBRARY OF CONGRESS CATALOGING-IN-PUBLICATION DATA

Hoffman, Nancy, 1955–
   Life after death / by Nancy Hoffman.
      p. cm. — (The mystery library)
Includes bibliographical references and index.
Contents: Where people go after they die—Reincarnation—Near Death Experiences—
Communication with the Dead.
   ISBN 1-59018-129-8
1. Future life--Juvenile literature. I. Title. II. Series: Mystery library (Lucent Books)
   BL535.H64 2004
   133.9'01'3—dc22

                   2004000385

Printed in the United States of America

Contents

Foreword

In Shakespeare's immortal play *Hamlet*, the young Danish aristocrat Horatio has clearly been astonished and disconcerted by his encounter with a ghostlike apparition on the castle battlements. "There are more things in heaven and earth," his friend Hamlet assures him, "than are dreamt of in your philosophy."

Many people today would readily agree with Hamlet, that the world and the vast universe surrounding it are teeming with wonders and oddities that remain largely outside the realm of present human knowledge or understanding. How did the universe begin? What caused the dinosaurs to become extinct? Was the lost continent of Atlantis a real place or merely legendary? Does a monstrous creature lurk beneath the surface of Scotland's Loch Ness? These are only a few of the intriguing questions that remain unanswered, despite the many great strides made by science in recent centuries.

Lucent Books' Mystery Library series is dedicated to exploring these and other perplexing, sometimes bizarre, and often disturbing or frightening wonders. Each volume in the series presents the best-known tales, incidents, and evidence surrounding the topic in question. Also included are the opinions and theories of scientists and other experts who have attempted to unravel and solve the ongoing mystery. And supplementing this information is a fulsome list of sources for further reading, providing the reader with the means to pursue the topic further.

The Mystery Library will satisfy every young reader's fascination for the unexplained. As one of history's greatest scientists, physicist Albert Einstein, put it:

> The most beautiful thing we can experience is the mysterious. It is the source of all true art and science. He to whom this emotion is a stranger, who can no longer wonder and stand rapt in awe, is as good as dead: his eyes are closed.

After We Die

Everyone dies. But what happens to people after they die has been questioned by humans since they first walked the earth. Modern science, which documents that the body shuts down when it dies, offers no clear evidence that any part of the dying person survives, yet few accept death as final. While some see death as a peaceful end to life, others believe that a joyful journey to a spiritual place, a rebirth into another life, or an eternity of punishment follows death. Many people, like the title character in William Shakespeare's play *Hamlet*, are baffled by the possibility of life after death.

> "To die, to sleep;
> To sleep: perchance to dream: ay, there's the rub;
> For in that sleep of death what dreams may come . . . ,"
> muses Hamlet.[1]

Most modern societies and traditional religions believe that when a person's body dies, his or her soul survives. The soul has been described as a person's spirit. It may be called a person's being, or essence. Sometimes it is said to be the conscience of an individual. To the ancient Greeks, the soul was even more important than the physical body. The Greeks believed the soul was trapped in the body and freed at death when the soul and body separated. That belief is echoed in a letter Elisabeth Kübler-Ross, the author of several books on death and dying, received from a child with cancer: "When we have done all the work we were sent to Earth to do, we are allowed to shed our body, which imprisons our soul like a cocoon encloses the future butterfly. And when the time is right, we can let go of it and we will be free of pain, free of fears and worries—free as a very beautiful butterfly, returning home to God."[2]

Ancient Artifacts and Beliefs

Although it cannot be proved, the idea of an afterlife has existed throughout history. Utensils, weapons, and other artifacts found at prehistoric burial sites indicate ancient peoples believed in life after death. The well-known researcher George Gallup Jr. wrote in *Adventures in Immortality*, "The earliest artists and craftsmen often made life after death a subject of their cave drawings or their pottery decorations. Every major religion has explored the possible landscape of an afterlife."[3]

Beliefs concerning life after death vary greatly. Some ancient cultures claimed death and the afterlife were like

Some people believe that a person's soul is released from the body at death, much like a butterfly is freed from its cocoon.

other cycles of nature. Just as flowers die in winter and come back in spring, people die and are reborn into new lives. In both African and Polynesian myths, human beings are thought to renew their lives like snakes regenerate their skin.

The ancient Egyptians considered life on Earth simply a preparation for the afterlife. Because they would spend eternity in their graves, they thought their graves more important than their homes, which were only temporary residences. When a new Egyptian ruler, or pharaoh, came to power, work immediately began on his tomb. The great Egyptian pyramids were built as elaborate mausoleums for pharaohs.

A few religions believe the soul does not go to another place after death. Originally, the Jewish faith proclaimed there was no afterlife; people's immortality came through the stories and physical attributes their children and their children's children inherited from them.

Modern Views of the Afterlife

Many fear death as they fear the unknown, while others see it not as an end but a beginning. However, most believe there is life after death—whether as ghosts haunting the places of their earthly lives or as spirits living in heavenly or hellish worlds. Statistics gathered by Gallup poll researchers in the 1980s and 1990s reveal most Americans (more than two-thirds) believe in life after death. Almost a quarter believe people are reborn again or reincarnated into new bodies, and another quarter of the U.S. population believes it is possible to communicate with the dead. People's beliefs of where or what the afterlife is vary greatly.

Chapter 1

Where Do People Go After They Die?

Most people who believe in a hereafter spend much of their lives in preparation for death and the afterlife. Many think how a person lived his or her life determines where they go after they die. Some religions contend individuals' thoughts, words, and deeds are judged after death. That judgment can take the form of weighing the heart as in ancient Egyptian society (heavy hearts hold more sins and more guilt) or reviewing a person's entire life. Whether the verdict was positive, negative, or in-between determines whether that individual spends an afterlife in a joyous state, in a frightening place, or waiting in limbo. If the soul does survive death, the afterlife may begin with a journey to the other side.

Simple Journeys to the Afterlife
Several cultures—from those of the ancient Egyptians and the ancient Aztecs to modern-day tribal societies—share beliefs that all the souls of the dead travel to an underworld

In this ancient Egyptian papyrus, the god of the dead Anubis weighs a man's heart to determine his lot in the afterlife. The Egyptians believed that sinners had heavy hearts.

to live out eternity. Some belief systems, such as many Native American religions, view death and the afterlife as simply part of life's endless journey. Human beings come from a spirit world, are born into earthly lives, and return to that spirit world when they die. Native Americans do not fear death but consider it part of the natural cycle of life. This belief is illustrated in the stories of the Tlingit peoples of Alaska. According to Tlingit mythology, salmon are people in animal form. Where the great rivers meet the sea, the salmon people shed their human clothes for fish scales and fins and swim upstream. When caught and eaten by the Tlingits, the salmon bones return to the sea where they turn back into salmon people. In these myths, cherishing the earth and its gifts are emphasized more than the afterlife or spirit world. "For the American Indians . . . , religion primarily serves the present life; it protects livelihood, health, and success," writes Ake Hultkrantz in *The Religions of the American Indians*. "The thought of life's termination is pushed aside."[4]

Because the Native American cycle of birth and death is continuous, it often requires traveling to the spirit world between lives. Those journeys are believed to be simple. Many tribes of the Great Plains believe their dead float up to the land of the Great Spirit like smoke from campfires; tribes in the southwestern United States believe their dead descend to underground or underwater villages; and the Cherokee believe that mystical rivers carry their dead to the afterlife.

Complex Journeys

In other cultures, voyages to the other side often include elaborate tests and feats to decide the soul's destiny. More complex and rigorous journeys require much preparation during one's lifetime. The ancient Egyptians believed the dead had a particularly complicated journey to the afterlife. According to ancient Egyptian texts, the newly dead sailed across the sky in a boat with the sun god, Ra. Upon landing in the west, the dead were required to pass through seven different gates each guarded by gatekeepers who questioned them about their lives. The last gate opens upon the hall of judgment where individual hearts are weighed. To the Egyptians, the heart was the center of the human conscience. They believed the more guilt people felt about their deeds in life, the heavier their heart would be when they died. Those with heavy hearts are put in a pit of fire until their hearts are lightened. Then they can join Osiris, the god of the dead, in his kingdom.

Many ancient Egyptians spent their entire lives preparing for their deaths. They stocked their tombs with whatever was needed, including food and drink, for a successful journey to the afterlife. This ancient civilization believed the dead would need their physical bodies for their voyage so they learned to preserve bodies through a process called mummification. The Egyptians also placed wooden replicas of the departed with the bodies and drew pictures depicting their lives on tomb walls for comfort. Most importantly, Egyptians left the deceased detailed instructions for a successful pilgrimage to the afterlife, including how to properly answer the seven gatekeepers' questions. Those instructions, known as the Egyptian Book of the Dead, were sometimes written out on long papyrus scrolls and placed within the burial chamber or etched into the lids of coffins called sarcophagi.

Ancient Egyptians practiced mummification in order to preserve their physical bodies for the arduous journey to the afterlife.

Crossing Rivers and Bridges

Many believe crossing mystical rivers is part of the journey to the afterlife. In ancient Greek mythology the dead cross

the River Styx, which separates the world of the living from Hades, the land of the dead that was ruled by a god of the same name. The newly departed needed a coin to pay a boatman named Charon to take them to the other side. So, to prepare for the river crossing, the ancient Greeks buried people with a coin in their mouths. Once across the river, the souls of the dead were judged. The heroes were sent to the land of light, known as Elysian

An elaborate sarcophagus lid from the Etruscan civilization, an early Italian people, covers the remains of a husband and wife.

Psyche, a mythological Greek princess, pays the boatman Charon to ferry her across the River Styx. On the other side of Styx, the souls of the dead were judged.

fields; the evil ones were left to suffer forever in a dreary underworld. The ancient Greek underworld was guarded by a ferocious three-headed dog named Cerberus who let the dead in but not out of the realm of Hades.

Zoroastrianism, an early religion that originated in what is now Iraq, held similar beliefs that souls must cross rivers in the afterlife to be judged. The Zoroastrians believed the dead must cross a bridge over a river of fire to learn their fate. As the souls of the departed walked over the Chinvat Bridge, it grew narrower and narrower until the center, where it was only the width of a sword's sharp edge. According to Zoroastrian beliefs, this is where judgment took place.

Hell is below the Bridge. Then the soul is carried to where stands a sword. If the soul is righteous, the sword presents its broad side. If the soul be wicked, that sword continues to stand edgewise, and does not give passage. With three steps which the soul takes forward—which are the evil thoughts, words, and deeds that it has performed—it is cut down from the head of the Bridge, and falls headlong to Hell.[5]

Those souls who were able to cross the Chinvat Bridge reached the underworld where they waited for resurrection.

Resurrection at the End of the World

Zoroastrianism and other religions, including Judaism, Christianity, and Islam, believed in resurrection, in which the dead remain in a lifeless limbo until the end of the world when a final judgment is given to all. In the Old Testament, Job, the hero of the book bearing his name, described this state of limbo as: "Man breathes his last, and where is he? As water fails from a lake, and a river wastes away and dries up, so man lies down and rises not again."[6]

The Zoroastrians taught that shortly before the end of the world, the prophet Zoroaster will appear on Earth and the final battle between the forces of good and evil will begin. On that last day, God will triumph. Then the living and all of the dead—including those in hell—will be judged, and those considered worthy will be reunited with their bodies. The newly resurrected join the rest of humanity in entering a new world full of peace and harmony. In Christianity, the righteous dead ascend to God's kingdom in heaven.

Judaism, Christianity, and Islam all adopted the Zoroastrian idea of final judgment and resurrection. However, the doctrines of those religions deal much more harshly with the souls in hell. Judaism's view of the end of the world is described in the prophecy of Daniel as: "Many of those that sleep in the dust of the earth shall awake, some to everlasting life, and some to shame and everlasting contempt."[7] Medieval Christian artifacts depict the Last Judgment as the day when each soul is weighed and Christ returns to Earth to condemn the wicked. Islam also proclaims the last day to be one of judgment and resurrection with Allah, their God, only restoring the righteous dead to life while the evil disintegrate.

Heaven As a Garden

Some religions believe that people who live a good life will go to a glorious heaven when they die. Different societies and even different sects of the same religions hold varying views of heaven, but it is generally thought to be a place full of love where all needs and desires are met. Many think the good and faithful can be closer to God there. For many believers, heaven cannot truly be described in words. In the New Testament book of Corinthians, people are not expected to understand what heaven will be like: "What no eye has seen, nor ear heard, nor the heart of man, conceived, what God has prepared for those who love him."[8]

Because heaven is difficult to imagine, some emphasize what heaven is not rather than what it is. Rabbi Rav, a Jewish scholar who preached in Babylonia in the third century, claimed in heaven there is "neither eating, nor drinking, nor any begetting of children, no bargaining or jealousy or hatred or strife. All that the righteous do is to sit with their crowns on their heads and enjoy the effulgence of the Presence."[9]

Ancient cultures usually believed this beautiful place was located above the earth. The ancient Egyptians ascended to a land resembling a cultivated Nile Valley, rich with fields of grain; ancient Greek heroes went up to Elysian fields, the land of light; and the ancient Aztecs traveled to the heavenly house of the sun. In an early Christian text, the prophet Levi claimed heaven is on a high mountaintop paradise: "I beheld a high mountain, and I was on it. And behold, the heavens were opened, and an angel of the Lord spoke to me: 'Levi, Levi, enter.' . . . And I saw the Most High sitting on a throne."[10]

Many people see heaven as a beautiful garden, bursting with orchards of ripe fruit, colorful flowers, and birds singing in the trees. They picture plenty of water flowing from waterfalls, mountain springs, and babbling brooks along with animals of every kind living in harmony. Heaven is often described as not of the earth but with all the pleasures of the earth. In 1978, Betty Eadie claimed to have visited heaven while she was on the brink of death. In her book *Embraced by the Light*, Eadie writes that while wandering through heaven she stopped to study the landscape: "The garden was filled with trees and flowers and plants. I walked on the grass for a time. It was crisp, cool and brilliant green and it felt alive under my feet. But what

Many cultures believe that heaven is a beautiful garden filled with flowing rivers, birds, trees, and flowers.

Some religions interpret heaven as a wondrous place where every person, animal, and plant live together in absolute harmony.

filled me with awe in the garden more than anything were the intense colors. We have nothing like them [on earth]."[11]

The Glorious City of Heaven

Heaven is often described as a wondrous city of light with beautiful translucent buildings of varying sizes and shapes and streets paved in gold. Arthur Ford, a man who believes he has been to heaven, marveled at the attitude of industrious souls in the book *The Eternal Journey*. "Everyone there was busy," he says. "They were continually occupied with mysterious errands and seemed to be very happy."[12]

According to the Old Testament, the prophet Enoch was the first person to visit heaven without dying. In the Book of Enoch, an ancient religious text accepted only in the Ethiopic Christian version of the Old Testament, Enoch's vision of heaven is given, starting at the door of a magnificent house of marble: "And I entered that house, and it was hot as fire and cold as snow, and there was neither pleasure nor life in it. Fear covered me and trembling took hold of me." Through an open door leading to an even more beautiful house, Enoch finds a being he recognizes as God.

> I saw in it a lofty throne, and its appearance was like crystal and its wheels like the shining sun. . . . And from underneath the lofty throne there flowed out rivers of burning fire so that it was impossible to look at it. And he who is great in glory sat on it, and his raiment was brighter than the sun, and whiter than any snow. . . . A sea of fire burnt around him and a great fire stood before him, and none of those around him came near to him.[13]

In most religions, what makes heaven so desirable is that its inhabitants can grow closer to God. Christian philosopher St. Thomas Aquinas portrayed heaven as the place where the faithful come, free from pain and sorrows, to live in bliss and know God. Many Christians, Muslims, and Jews do not think of heaven as a place but rather a state of mind in which people better understand God by experiencing his love. That understanding is believed to be the true blessing of heaven.

Hell

Some religions hold that the souls of humans who have been selfish and cruel go to hell, a place of eternal damnation. But hell did not start out being as horrible as it was later perceived. The word *hell* comes from Hel, the name of a goddess of the dead. According to Scandinavian mythology, Hel ruled the underworld where people went after they died. Hel's domain was neither frightening nor gloomy. Likewise, old Jewish tradition dictates all of the dead—the good and the bad—end up in the same dark and lonely place, Sheol. As Christianity spread throughout Europe during the Middle Ages, the idea of spending eternity in heaven for living a good life grew along with an increasingly negative view of hell, which became associated with fire and horrible suffering—a place to be avoided at all costs.

Other ancient religions, like Hinduism, have described hell as a dark place where dust is food and clay is meat. In Hinduism, hell is reserved for only the most vile human souls—those who are so evil they will not even be reincarnated, or reborn into another life, as Hindus believe most people are. The Chinese view hell as a place where evildoers are imprisoned and tortured. But this hell is not eternal; the Chinese hold that souls eventually leave hell and are reincarnated into new lives. Geddes MacGregor writes about the Chinese view of hell in his book *Images of Afterlife*, "It lacks the awful hopelessness of the Christian hell; nevertheless, being continuously skinned alive for even a year or two is terrifying enough."[14]

The ancient Greeks believed that Hades, the god of the underworld, ruled over a gloomy realm inhabited by ghostly wisps of dead souls. While there is no suffering in Hades' kingdom, the dead forget the pleasures of life once they drink water from Lethe, a mystical spring. Similarly, the ancient Jewish hell, Sheol, is a place where the dead forget life and even forget God.

In most religions the threat of eternal damnation deters bad behavior. In 1893, R.F. Clarke, a priest in Oxford, England, wrote: "The fear of hell is a powerful deterrent to many educated as well as uneducated, and many a sin

A detail from a medieval painting shows Satan devouring the worst sinners at the bottom of hell, while sinners guilty of lesser crimes endure torments at the hands of demons.

would be committed were it not for the wholesome dread of eternal misery before the sinner's eyes."[15] A nineteenth-century Roman Catholic priest named Furniss wrote books to teach children about the horrors of hell. In his book *Visions of Heaven and Hell*, Richard Cavendish describes Furniss's stories. In one, "A 16 year old girl who preferred going to the park on Sunday to going to church is condemned to stand eternally barefooted on a red-hot floor." In another, "A boy who drank and kept bad company is permanently immersed in a boiling kettle."[16] These stories kept many from behaving badly. In effect, fear of an unpleasant life after death can affect how people live their lives.

Many Heavens and Many Hells

The idea of one heaven and one hell does not account for people who have committed bad deeds but do not necessarily deserve to suffer in a hell as harsh as Furniss described. To distinguish between how good or bad a person is, many religions believe in several different levels of both heaven and hell. Doctrines of the Mormon Church claim three levels of heaven, one for the completely righteous, one for those who were good but did not accept the teachings of the Mormon Church, and the third for those who were sinful (since Mormons do not believe in hell). Islam's heaven and hell have seven layers each. How good or how bad a person was in life determines which level of heaven or hell they enter upon death.

According to the Koran, the holy book of Islam, Allah created seven heavens lying outside the realm of human time and space. The heavens emphasize different versions of paradise —one is a land of peace, another is full of earthly delights, and another like a beautiful garden. According to the Koran the heavenly garden is full of trees providing unlimited fruit and shade and rivers of water, milk, wine, and honey. Since much of the Muslim world is located in a hot, dry climate, it is understandable why unlimited food, drink, and a pleasant climate are part of the Islamic garden paradise.

The ancient Aztecs of Mexico also claimed many heavens existed. However, Aztec heavens were not created to reward different levels of righteousness but rather as places for souls with different needs. Warriors or those who were sacrificed in religious rituals went to one heaven. Women who died giving birth had their own paradise. And those who drowned or died from diseases associated with water went to the most desirable realm of the Aztec rain god, who was important because he was responsible for helping crops grow and sustaining life.

Purgatory

Purgatory is a second chance for the souls of people who are considered neither good nor bad. It is a Christian doctrine accepted by Roman Catholic and Eastern Orthodox churches. The word *purgatory* means purification, and that is what souls must undergo before they are allowed to enter the kingdom of heaven.

Many Catholics believe purgatory is a chilly waiting room where people purify their souls by looking in a mirror and confronting their bad thoughts and deeds. Others believe the process of going through purgatory means being consumed by fire. In the thirteenth century, when the Roman Catholic Church first accepted the idea of purgatory, it described the experience as: "There is a purgatorial fire in which the souls of the pious are purified by the temporary punishment so that an entrance may be opened for them into the eternal country in which nothing stained can enter."[17]

Two hundred years later, St. Catherine of Genoa presumed many souls can choose the particular kind of purgatory they wanted or needed to progress spiritually. Most, however, picked fire as a way to purify their soul. According to this fifteenth-century saint, as the soul burned, the pain of the fire is eventually replaced with joy—the joy of seeing and accepting God. At that point, the soul may enter heaven.

Many religions believe that those who are not baptized or do not believe in God cannot go to heaven. To its believers, the doctrine of purgatory offers more positive explanations for what happens to babies not baptized and others who die before developing a belief in God.

Dante's Vision of the Afterlife

Perhaps the most comprehensive account of heaven, hell, and purgatory comes from the medieval Italian poet,

A baby is baptized using holy water. Many religions believe people who are not baptized cannot go to heaven.

philosopher, and theologian Dante Alighieri, who combined both ancient Greek and Christian beliefs in describing the afterlife. Dante's description of the universe, given in his epic poem, *The Divine Comedy*, was much more specific than the Bible it supported. Written as if the poet is taking a tour of the afterlife, Dante's account was so detailed that some people of his time thought Dante actually visited heaven, hell, and purgatory. His work provided a basis for many beliefs about the places people go after they die.

Dante wrote about hell as a cone divided into nine sections with its tip at the center of the earth. Vile creatures of all kinds inhabit Dante's hell including Cerberus, a three-headed dog of Greek and Roman mythology. The different levels house the souls of different kinds of sinners. For example, levels two through four include those who are guilty of offenses such as anger and gluttony, the sixth level is for heretics, and the eighth level for those who committed fraud and malice against others. At the ninth level is the frozen lake where Lucifer (the devil) dwells as a frosty monster.

A path from the center of the earth extends to purgatory, which is a mountain formed on the other side of Earth. On the mountain are seven flaming terraces, each corresponding to the seven deadly sins of Christianity. A soul can purge himself of sins by climbing the mountain to St. Peter's gate to heaven. This gate is accessible through the last flaming wall of purgatory.

In Dante's universe, nine concentric circles revolve above the earth. Within each circle is one of nine heavens ruled by one of nine orders of angels. The heavens spin around a brilliant light in the center, which is God. Dante described the light: "Within Its depthless clarity of substance I saw the Great Light shine into three circles. In three clear colors bound in one same space."[18] The three

Dante Alighieri intricately describes his vision of heaven, purgatory, and hell in his epic poem The Divine Comedy.

DANTE ALIGIER CIT TA DIN FIORETINO
POETA·ACVTISSIMO·ET·DIVINO 2010

circles symbolize the Father, Son, and Holy Ghost of the Christian Trinity.

While Judaism, Christianity, and Islam, among other religions, teach that souls spend eternity in heaven or hell, most of the world's population does not believe people go to a physical place after they die. The majority of people hold that the dead are reborn into other human lives.

Chapter 2

Reincarnation

Reincarnation is the belief that a soul is born into another body after death for the purpose of learning and growing spiritually. Most think reincarnation's cycle of birth, death, and rebirth includes hundreds of lifetimes. Old souls bring many experiences into each new life, although generally, people cannot consciously remember them. Early-twentieth-century English author Rider Haggard explained this phenomenon: "The Personality which animates each one of us is immeasurably ancient, having been forged in many fires."[19]

According to a 1981 Gallup poll, approximately two-thirds of the world's population believes in reincarnation. This theory is a major part of religions practiced in Asia—the two most common being Hinduism and Buddhism, both of which originated in India. Other believers include members of modern tribal societies in Africa and Australia and a growing number of people in the Western Hemisphere.

Karma

In the Hindu and Buddhist views of reincarnation, lessons are learned over many lifetimes. Karma is a natural law that proclaims every good deed is eventually rewarded while bad deeds are punished, whether in that lifetime or a future one. The quality of one's life is determined by the soul's karma. Young Buddhists and Hindus learn that how they behaved in past lives determines what their present life is like and how they behave in this life will affect subsequent lives. The Dalai Lama, the spiritual leader of

Tibetan Buddhists, believes the law of karma is "a very practical approach because it places firmly in our own hands responsibility for the kind of person we are now and the kind of person we may become."[20]

People who believe in reincarnation are encouraged to build up good karma, progressing to higher spiritual levels with each life. According to Buddhist monk Rimpoche Nawang Gehlek, good and bad karma accumulated over several lifetimes creates a pattern of experiences that subconsciously influences an individual. What an individual learns in one lifetime might not be used until another lifetime. For example, being poor in one lifetime might teach a person the importance of being charitable when they are reincarnated into a more prosperous lifetime.

Similarly problems arising in one lifetime might not be resolved until a future lifetime. In her book *Return to Heaven*, Carol Bowman writes about several parents who claim their children are their reincarnated relatives. In one case, Bowman describes a woman who believes her young daughter is actually the reincarnated soul of her alcoholic mother. The woman first suspected her child's past life when the girl referred to herself by her deceased grandmother's nickname—a nickname the young daughter could not possibly know. Later the daughter told her mother, "I didn't like you very much when you were my little girl." Startled, the mother asked, "Why didn't you? Mommies always love their little girls?" The girl replied, "Because you always used to yell at me, and push me into my room and lock the door." The woman was dumbfounded because she remembered times when she screamed at her mother and locked her into her room when her mother was drunk and abusive. Bowman believes the soul of the abusive mother was reincarnated into her own granddaughter to resolve the problems created in her earlier life.[21]

Individuals can also accumulate negative karma, which accounts for suffering in future lives. As Gehlek writes in

Good Life, Good Death, "Bad actions lead to more suffering and to a lack of freedom and that's why it's so important for us to correct our negative habits."[22] Both Hindus and Buddhists claim those who have degraded themselves and others develop bad karma and could return to Earth in the body of an animal or even a plant.

Tibetan Buddhist monks chant prayers as non-Buddhists look on. Buddhists believe in a karmic cycle of death and rebirth known as samsara.

Samsara

The cycle of accumulating good and bad karma seems endless. In Hindu and Buddhist traditions, the cycle of death and rebirth is known as samsara. Buddhists and Hindus strive to escape the cycle, for that is the only way to reach spiritual peace. According to Buddhist teachings, life's mistakes and misdeeds create a web restricting an individual's spiritual growth. Re-creating bad karma limits the soul's

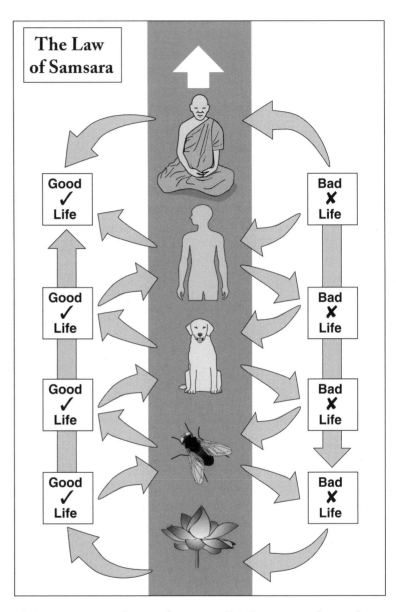

ability to move forward spiritually. Learning from those mistakes and achieving only good karma from one life to another frees the soul. As written in the Rig-Veda, a Hindu holy book, through samara the soul can "leave sin and evil, seek anew the dwelling, and bright with glory wear another body."[23]

Nirvana

Buddhists who are released from the cycle of samsara enter nirvana, which is often thought of as the Buddhist form of heaven. Nirvana is not, however, a place like most heavens described in Christianity, Judaism, or Islam. It is a state of being in which one is free of all earthly values and desires, which prevent a person from growing spiritually and finding true peace. In *Images of Afterlife*, Geddes MacGregor describes nirvana, which literally means extinction, as what "one might say of a candle the light of which has been blown out." Nirvana is the extinguishment of what MacGregor refers to as "the ignorant cravings in which human misery is rooted. The state of nirvanic bliss is one that may be likened to the joy of having learned truths that explain what had been the cause of one's misery."[24]

In his book *Good Life, Good Death*, Buddhist monk Rimpoche Nawang Gehlek describes how a fellow monk named Gomo Rimpoche helped one dying man release his desires, allowing him to grow closer to reaching nirvana. The monk had trained the man in meditation, but at the time of his death, he felt intense pain and anxiety. Gomo Rimpoche noticed the man greatly valued the new shirt he was wearing. Believing the man's attachment to the shirt, a material desire, prevented him from seeking enlightenment, the monk demanded the man give him the shirt. After some relenting, the man did as Gomo Rimpoche asked. Then the monk ripped the man's shirt to shreds. After some initial shock, the man's pain and anxiety seemed to slip away as he died, peacefully.

Reincarnated Spiritual Teachers

Like the ancient Greeks believed the dead drank water making them forget their former life, Buddhists and Hindus believe most people are unaware of their past lives. However, many claim those who are highly evolved spiritually do remember former lives. For those individuals samsara is an opportunity to continue good work on earth. Lamas are Tibetan spiritual teachers who escape samsara and could go on to nirvana when they die but choose to be reborn into earthly lives to help others find enlightenment. Because they are so highly evolved spiritually, lamas often remember their past lives.

Tibetan Buddhist priests have found children believed to be reincarnated lamas all over the world, including the United States, New Zealand, France, Spain, and several other Western countries. After the death of the Dalai Lama,

Hindus bathe in an Indian river to purify themselves. Hindus believe that such ritual purification is essential to releasing oneself from the cycle of samsara.

The fourteenth Dalai Lama meditates during a visit to India. Tibetan Buddhists believe the Dalai Lama is reincarnated as a child following the previous lama's death.

the supreme lama and leader of Tibetan Buddhists, a group of Tibetan spiritual teachers search the world to find the child who they believe is the reincarnation of the Dalai Lama. The current Dalai Lama, believed to be the fourteenth reincarnation of the Tibetan spiritual leader, was born in 1933. At the death of the last Dalai Lama, the interim leader of Tibetan Buddhists had a vision about a small house with turquoise tiles. The garden of the house was full of peach blossoms, and there was a woman holding a baby boy. The visionary believed the infant to be the new Dalai Lama. Led by this vision, a Tibetan council of lamas found the boy and determined he was their leader by having the child identify the simple possessions of the deceased Dalai Lama.

Other Forms of Reincarnation

Not all human beings are reborn as people, according to many beliefs. Some ancient Greeks believed people could reincarnate into animals. Some modern Western groups believing in reincarnation claim everything from rocks to plants to animals have souls, and reincarnation is the process of spiritual evolution that souls go through before they are granted lives as human beings.

Many beliefs in reincarnation do not include karma, samsara, or nirvana. Some see reincarnation as a form of ancestor worship in which people are reincarnated into their descendants. Many tribes in western and southern Africa consider it evil not to be reborn into the same family. Those couples who remain childless are poorly regarded for not honoring their ancestors by providing them with bodies for their new earthly lives. Similarly, many of Australia's aboriginal tribes believe souls of dead ancestors are reborn as their descendants. In this belief, the reincarnation process often begins with the spirit of an ancestor inhabiting an inanimate object or monument. The ancestor's soul then enters the body of a mother at the moment of conception.

Déjà Vu As Evidence of Reincarnation

People claim to find evidence of reincarnation often. Many believe sensing something strongly familiar about someone they just met is proof of reincarnation. That feeling of familiarity about a person, place, or event is called déjà vu. According to the late Elisabeth Kübler-Ross, a psychiatrist who has written about helping the terminally ill and their families deal with death, that feeling of déjà vu often

involves "a sense of recognizing a place and being totally aware of details in a way that no one could explain scientifically." Generally, she believes, when people experience that feeling of familiarity when meeting someone new it is often the result of having known that person in a past life because it seems "as if they had known each other for decades and not just for a brief moment. And they often say jokingly, 'Maybe we have been together in another lifetime.' If they only knew how true this is in many cases."[25]

The psychiatrist who founded analytical psychology, Carl Jung, experienced a profound sense of déjà vu while traveling in Africa in the 1920s. Jung was so moved by the feeling of familiarity that it influenced much of his later work. Jung wrote of it:

> The train, swathed in a red cloud of dust, was just making a turn around a steep red cliff. On a jagged rock above us a slim, brownish-black figure stood motionless, leaning on a long spear, looking down at the train. Beside him towered a gigantic candelabrum cactus. I had the feeling that I had already

Australian Aborigines participate in a ritual dance. Many aboriginal tribes believe the souls of dead ancestors are reborn as their descendants.

experienced this moment and had always known this world which was separated from me only by distance in time. It was as if I were at this moment returning to the land of my youth, and as if I knew that dark-skinned man who had been waiting for me for five thousand years.[26]

The problem with déjà vu as evidence of reincarnation is that it is impossible to prove scientifically. Still, many people claim their strong déjà vu feelings are proof enough.

Past-Life Memories

Other unscientific proof of reincarnation has come from people who claim to remember former lives. Several cases over the past 150 years have been investigated. Often these memories are uncovered when a person is hypnotized, since hypnosis helps people relax and focus on what they are asked to remember. One of the most famous cases came to light in 1952 when twenty-nine-year-old housewife Virginia Tighe was hypnotized in Pueblo, Colorado. Hypnotist Morey Bernstein urged his subject to go back farther and farther in time until she began speaking with an Irish brogue and calling herself Bridey Murphy. Under hypnosis, Tighe, who had never lived nor traveled outside of the United States, claimed she was born Bridget Kathleen Murphy in 1798 in County Cork, Ireland. As Bridey Murphy, Tighe said her father was a lawyer named Duncan Murphy and her husband a teacher named Sean Brian Joseph MacCarthy. Tighe also claimed that as Bridey Murphy, she died at age sixty-six in Belfast, Ireland. Bernstein's 1956 book about the case, *The Search for Bridey Murphy*, became an instant best-seller and spawned an interest in reincarnation nationwide, despite the fact that investigations into Tighe's claims could never prove that a Bridey Murphy had been born in 1798.

Similarly, other cases of past-life memories gained notoriety. In Wales, a woman named Jane Evans consulted

Under hypnosis, Virginia Tighe (holding child) claimed she was the reincarnation of an eighteenth-century Irish woman named Bridey Murphy.

with hypnotherapist Arnall Bloxham, hoping he could cure her rheumatism. Under hypnosis, Evans talked about seven past lives, including one as a young woman who died in the 1190 massacre of Jews in York, England. A York University expert on the history of English Jews studied the tape recording of Evans's sessions. He found the information Evans gave about Jewish life in the late twelfth century in England to be accurate and not widely known except by professional historians.

Past-Life Therapy

As more news reports of past-life memories surfaced, more psychiatrists experimented with urging patients to regress back to before they were born in an effort to help them cope with various phobias and neuroses. Many psychiatrists believe an adult's problems can be traced back to forgotten childhood traumas. Using hypnosis, psychiatrists can bring patients back to childhood and make them aware of when and how their problems started. That awareness helps patients better understand and deal with their problems.

A few psychiatrists believe some problems result from traumatic situations experienced in past lives and that regressing patients back to those past lives helps them better cope with the present. That procedure is called past-life therapy. Such therapy is regarded as highly suspect by many in the psychiatric community, who generally believe the memories produced from past-life therapy are simply illusions that mask real childhood trauma. Despite the controversy, at least one well-respected psychotherapist has shown some success with it.

As chief of psychiatry at a large university-affiliated hospital in Miami, Florida, Brian Weiss came upon the practice of past-life therapy quite by accident. A woman who worked at the hospital came to Weiss needing help dealing with a number of phobias. Under hypnosis, the woman began to recall several past lives. Most of her memories were filled with trauma and tragedy—she recounted being a leper cast out from a village, a victim of a flood, and a Spanish prostitute, among many other lives.

While Weiss does not necessarily believe the woman's past-life memories are proof of reincarnation, he cannot deny hypnotherapy was extremely successful in her case. "In just a few short months, her symptoms disappeared, and she resumed her life happier and more at peace than ever before,"[27] writes Weiss, who continued to successfully treat many more patients with past-life therapy. Some claim the memories of Weiss's patients and the fact that past-life therapy has worked prove reincarnation is real, while others disagree. Many are unsure what past-life memories are or mean.

Discovering Old Souls

Some anecdotal evidence of reincarnation is found without regressing into past lives through hypnosis. Some people—and not necessarily those deemed to be highly spiritually evolved—have claimed memories of past lives since they were children.

Since she was a very young child, Englishwoman Jenny Cockell has had recurring dreams about her death in an Irish hospital in the 1930s. In the dream, she was a mother named Mary Sutton who felt enormous guilt over dying and leaving her young children alone. "Mary died twenty-one years before I was born but memories of her life and of that time were always a part of me, shaping and affecting the person I grew to become,"[28] writes Cockell in her book *Across Time and Death: A Mother's Search for Her Past Life Children.*

The closer Cockell approached the age at which she believed Mary died (early to middle thirties), the more anxious she became and the more determined she was to learn about her former life and especially what happened to her past-life children. She began investigating and found Mary's birth and death certificates, confirming that Mary Sutton had lived in the early twentieth century. Eventually Cockell visited the town she claimed she once lived in and located five of Mary's eight children, who accepted her as at least having some psychic connection with their late mother. Like Cockell, others have researched claims of past lives. One professor of psychiatry at the University of Virginia has made a career out of such research.

A doctor hypnotizes a patient. Many people believe past-life memories can be brought to light through the use of hypnosis.

Ian Stevenson is known as the foremost expert in reincarnation research, having conducted it for the past forty years. Stevenson thinks his discoveries confirm at least the possibility that reincarnation exists. In Tom Shroder's book *Old Souls*, Stevenson wonders why mainstream scientists refuse to accept the evidence of reincarnation. Stevenson documented more than two thousand cases of children who believed they were reincarnated, including a two-year-old Lebanese boy who claimed to have had a previous life as a mechanic who died in a car crash. Relatives of the deceased mechanic believed the boy because he instantly recognized and named the mechanic's sister.

While much of Stevenson's research has been conducted in developing countries in which beliefs in reincarnation are more readily accepted, the professor has found several cases in the United States as well. In suburban Virginia a young boy insisted he owned a farm complete with cows and a shed. One day when out for a drive with his parents, the boy shouted out they were on the same road as his farm. The road curved and there was an old farmhouse with cows grazing in fields nearby and a shed beyond a small grove of trees.

Carol Bowman has also investigated several cases of children remembering past lives. She has found many children who believe they are the reincarnations of deceased relatives. Bowman writes of a young girl named Brittany who believes she is the reincarnation of her mother's deceased twin brother. Once Brittany told her grandmother, "Mommy doesn't 'member when I was in your tummy." Brittany's mother tried to correct the girl. But Brittany insisted, "No, before that when I was in Meemaw's tummy with you, Mommy. I couldn't stay because I didn't want to be a boy." The mother and grandmother were shocked because when the grandmother was pregnant with Brittany's mother, she had a twin brother who died seven months into the pregnancy.[29]

Collective Unconscious

However compelling the research of people like Stevenson, Cockell, and Bowman, many believe there are other explanations for the phenomena of past-life memories. In the 1920s, the pioneering Swiss psychiatrist Carl Jung seemed to have embraced the idea of reincarnation. After his déjà vu experience in Africa he wrote, "I could not guess what string within myself was plucked at by the sight of that solitary dark hunter. I knew only that his world had been mine for countless millennia."[30] However, out of that experience and others like it, Jung developed a theory known as collective unconscious that offered an alternative explanation for reincarnation. Collective unconscious refers to the history of mankind and the universal myths and symbols that can be found in most of the world's cultures. Jung believed the similarity of ancient stories of creation, powerful deities, death, and the afterlife proved that all human beings share some spiritual qualities.

Jung's theory also suggests that within each individual's collective unconscious are memories of ancestors. Jung believed those memories become part of every person's genetic code and all people inherit some of the individual, personal recollections from all of their ancestors. Jung thought that people who think they are recalling past lives are actually tapping into their collective unconscious.

Active Imaginations?

Many people believe past-life memories are nothing more than the result of active imaginations. Countless people have thought they were famous people in other lives. In fact, some famous people believed they were also famous in other lifetimes. The late movie star Lana Turner was convinced she was once Cleopatra. World War II general George Patton believed he was the reincarnation of the brilliant military strategist Hannibal, who won many battles against the Romans between 218 B.C. and 216 B.C. Perhaps these people simply long to be more like their heroes. Many believe Virginia Tighe developed her memories of being Bridey Murphy from the stories of a neighbor. In the 1950s, a Chicago newspaper reported that as a child in Wisconsin, Tighe lived across the street from an Irish immigrant named Bridie Corkell.

Few people profess to have lived ordinary past lives. That is one of the main reasons Brian Weiss believed his first patient who recounted her past lives in their hypnosis sessions together. Tom Shroder writes about Weiss in his book *Old Souls*, "What convinced him that she was remembering actual past lives was that the lives themselves were so mundane."[31] However, skeptics point out that Weiss dismissed inconsistencies of his patient's past-life memories. For example, two of her incarnations apparently occurred at the same time.

Other Explanations for Past-Life Memories

Some believe people subconsciously take on past-life memories from historical books they have read or documentaries they have seen. Skeptics often question the mental health and honesty of the people claiming to remember past lives. Most psychiatrists do not necessarily believe patients are lying or mentally unstable. Often past-life recollections occur under hypnosis, and people are susceptible to suggestions of therapists in this state. For example, if a therapist asks a hypnotized patient to regress back to a former life, the patient might then create stories about a life they never really lived, just to fulfill the therapist's request. Furthermore,

Swiss psychiatrist Carl Jung theorized that within the individual's collective unconscious are memories of ancestors.

many psychiatrists believe what is described under hypnosis is not necessarily real. Psychiatrist Martin Orne told author Tom Shroder: "Hypnosis can create pseudo-memories. Reincarnation memories are no different than the cases of people who under hypnosis relate being captured by UFO space aliens and examined aboard the mother ship. These are what I call 'honest liars.'"[32]

Weiss's first patient who recalled past lives would agree with Orne. As a practicing Roman Catholic, she does not accept the doctrine of reincarnation and does not believe her memories are real, although she is grateful past-life therapy cured her.

The late movie star Lana Turner believed that she had been Egyptian queen Cleopatra in a past life.

Similarly some of Mary Sutton's children do not believe Jenny Cockell is the reincarnation of their mother. They do think Jenny's dreams of their mother's life were an important catalyst in bringing the Sutton children back together (most went to separate orphanages after their mother's death). However that reunion happened, they are grateful for it.

Balancing Science with Religion

Whether real or imagined, the phenomena of past-life memories are worth researching further say many therapists. As quoted in David Darling's book *Soul Search*, the Dalai Lama believes scientists and spiritual leaders can work together, especially when investigating beliefs about death, dying, and the afterlife: "Death and dying provide a meeting point between Tibetan Buddhist and modern scientific traditions. I believe both have a great deal to contribute to each other on the level of understanding and of practical benefit."[33]

Whatever beliefs people have concerning the afterlife, the idea of reincarnation comforts those who fear leaving loved ones forever after they die, those who hope for second chances to repair relationships, or those who refuse to think of death as the end.

Chapter 3

Near-Death Experiences

Perhaps the most compelling evidence of life after death are the accounts of people who die and are revived minutes later. Advances in medicine over the last century allow doctors to bring a growing number of people back to life after they have died. According to research from the International Association for Near Death Studies (IANDS), approximately one-third of those resuscitated individuals report having had some kind of near-death experience in which they felt they began the journey to an afterlife. A near-death experience, or NDE, can include the sensation of leaving the body, speeding through a dark tunnel toward a bright light, meeting deceased loved ones, visiting either a heavenly place or shadowy hell, and experiencing a detailed life review—all before being revived.

One reason most researchers believe NDE accounts are authentic is many near-death survivors find the experience difficult to explain to their families or medical personnel. Because NDEs are so profound, they are difficult to describe and many survivors fear people will not believe them or will think they are mentally ill. Despite that fact, the number of documented NDEs is growing. Some believe that is because medical technology allows more people to be resuscitated; others think people are slowly becoming more comfortable talking about mystical and spiritual experiences.

While each documented NDE is different all seem to share at least some similar aspects. The documentation gathered from reported NDEs is only anecdotal, but it is the best evidence yet for life after death. Almost all survivors say their NDE began with an out-of-body experience in which the soul leaves the body.

Out of the Body

In 1918, the famous American novelist Ernest Hemingway experienced what many believe was an out-of-body experience after being wounded by shrapnel in Italy during World War I. While recovering in a Milan hospital, he wrote his family: "Dying is a very simple thing. I've looked at death and . . . know." In an out-of-body experience, the

Many people recount racing through a tunnel toward a bright light during near-death experiences (NDEs).

person suddenly feels all pain and discomfort slip away as he or she leaves the body and floats up to view the scene of his or her death. It appears Hemingway had such an experience, but it took many years before he wrote about what happened to him:

> A big Austrian trench mortar bomb, of the type that used to be called ash cans exploded in the darkness. I died then. I felt my soul or something coming right out of my body, like you'd pull a silk handkerchief out of a pocket by one corner. It flew around and then came back and went in again and I wasn't dead anymore.[34]

Hemingway seemed to be profoundly changed by this NDE. Although he had always been tough and unsentimental before, Hemingway's family and friends agreed that he was "never again as hard-boiled as he once had been."[35]

Some people who have had near-death experiences recall leaving their earthly bodies and floating up toward heaven.

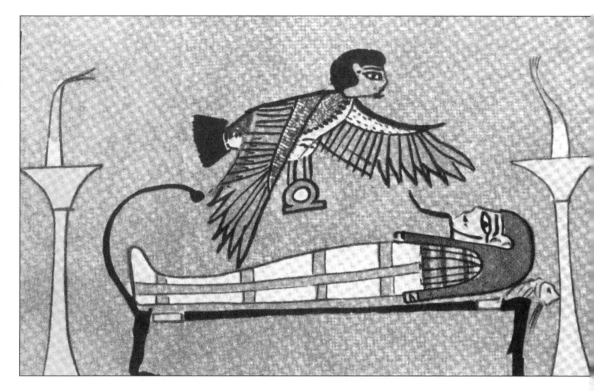

One of the first books documenting research about NDEs was Raymond Moody's *Life After Life*. Moody interviewed a man who at the age of seventeen nearly drowned after swimming out to the middle of a lake. The man, who says he slipped out of his body, described his view: "I saw my body in the water about three or four feet away, bobbling up and down. I viewed my body from the back and slightly to the right side. I still felt as though I had an entire body form, even while I was outside my body. I had an airy feeling that's almost indescribable. I felt like a feather."[36]

One subject Moody studied likened his NDE's out-of-body experience to being in another dimension: "Well, when I was taking geometry, they always told me there were only three dimensions, and I always just accepted that. But they were wrong. There are more."[37]

While in that other dimension, people may see the medical procedures used to save their lives. In research

An Egyptian papyrus depicts the soul of a man leaving his dead body in the form of a bird with the head of a man. The bird's claws clench a symbol of eternity.

done by Atlanta cardiologist Michael Sabom, patients who reported having NDEs accurately described how they were brought back from the brink of death. Some of Sabom's patients gave correct accounts of specific details such as the kind of gurneys they were on, the shape of defibrillator paddles used in resuscitation attempts, and the reactions of family members in the hospital waiting room.

The Tunnel

Most people claiming to have had an NDE report that they traveled through a dark tunnel. Accounts of the tunnel vary greatly. Moody's research in the 1970s illustrates these differences. One subject recalls an NDE he had at nine years old that started out with a rhythmic ringing noise. "I was moving through this—long dark place. It seemed like a sewer or something. I was moving, beating all the time with this noise, this ringing noise."[38] Another person interviewed by Moody remembered the experience as speeding through a black vacuum: "I felt like I was riding on a roller coaster train at an amusement park, going through this tunnel at a tremendous speed."[39] Most people feel wonderful and free of worry within the darkness of the tunnel.

Melvin Morse, a Seattle pediatrician who studies children's NDEs, documented reports from children and from adults who experienced NDEs when they were children. One woman interviewed by Morse told him she felt as if she traveled through the tunnel on water: "She said she was making her way through this mystical river in a small boat. The water was dark, but she was unafraid. Suddenly, she turned on to another branch of the river and passed under a glowing arch that led to a light."[40]

The Light

According to most NDE accounts, at the end of the tunnel there is a light that seems to be the most important and most memorable part of the NDE. In Melvin Morse's

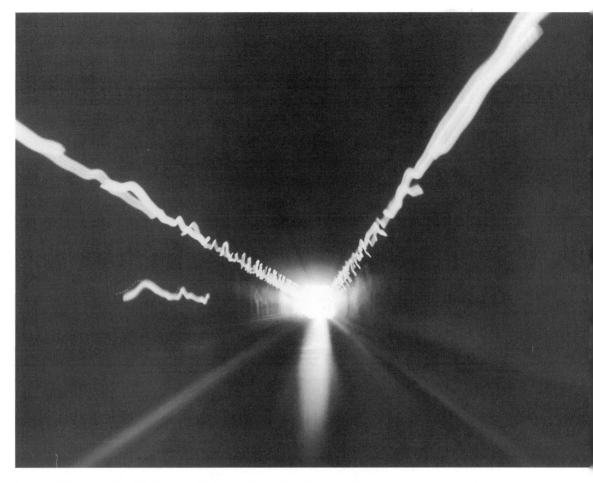

book *Closer to the Light*, the light is described by survivors as misty, glowing, or bright. A woman quoted in P.M.H. Atwater's book *Beyond the Light* likened it to "a very strong white light bulb that somehow did not hurt her eyes."[41] Others report it is a bright golden or soft pink light.

However people see it, the light is almost always thought of as pure unconditional love to which people are drawn. Many of Morse's patients have called the light "all-knowing," "all-forgiving," and "all-loving."[42] A woman named Terry said it was "so beautiful that it couldn't be called just a light. It represented love and peace and happiness and complete and utter joy."[43]

Many believe that the light at the end of the tunnel commonly seen by people who have had near-death experiences represents the unconditional love of God.

Some believe the light plays an active role in bringing them back to life. Morse became open to that possibility after hearing the stories of one eight-year-old patient named June who almost drowned and that of the man who saved her life. June slipped out of a boat and into the sandy bottom of Puget Sound near Seattle. Immediately a close family friend jumped in to save her. The cloudy day and cold, murky waters made the search difficult. The man resurfaced and dove back down to the bottom again and again. On the fourth try, he saw June's body. He said it seemed to be "illuminated from within by a soft bright light" that gave him "a sense of awe and reverence."[44] He managed to pull the girl's body out of the depths and she was rushed to the hospital. June made a complete recovery despite the fact she was under the water for nearly twenty minutes. Later, the man who saved her dove back into the sound but could not find the source of the mysterious light. Morse believes June was in the midst of an NDE and that both she and her rescuer simultaneously saw the light.

Another of Morse's subjects claims the light itself saved her from drowning when she was twelve years old. Deep in the water she saw the light and tried reaching for it: "But before I had a chance to touch it, I was transported to the shore. I know I wasn't swimming to the shore. The Light picked me up and took me there."[45]

Spiritual Guides

Some see mystical beings, or spiritual guides, in the light. In fact, most people who claim to have had NDEs say they did not go through the experience alone. Spiritual guides comforted them and allowed them to decide whether to return to their physical bodies and their earthly lives.

Katie had a childhood NDE after nearly drowning in a community swimming pool in Idaho. Because she did not have a pulse for nineteen minutes, the hospital staff was not certain whether she would awake from her coma.

When she awoke three days later and her pediatrician asked what she remembered while she was unconscious, Katie told him about a golden-haired angel named Elizabeth. Elizabeth took Katie by the hand and said she was there to help Katie. Together, they traveled to see Katie's brothers playing with their toys and her mother making a hasty dinner before hurrying back to her daughter's bedside; then Elizabeth took Katie to meet God. When Katie wished to see her mother again, she immediately woke from her coma. Surprised by this story, Katie's doctor asked her what it was like "up there." Katie simply replied, "Heaven is fun!"[46]

Unlike Katie's guide, spiritual guides are usually familiar to the person experiencing an NDE. People generally see their spiritual guides in terms of their particular backgrounds, cultures, and religions. Christians often see Jesus, St. Peter, or even the Archangel Gabriel, who tell them to go back because they have unfinished business. Hindus tend to view spiritual guides as messengers. Sometimes those messengers look over a long list of names and tell the person they have to return to Earth because they are not on the roster.

Many people believe their spiritual guides to be the souls of departed loved ones. People have reported meeting dead relatives such as grandparents, aunts, and brothers-in-law during their NDEs. A few claim to have met celebrities on the other side. One Canadian man told NDE researcher Kenneth Ring he saw the famous physicist Albert Einstein working on a computer in heaven. Elvis Presley is such a popular figure in accounts of NDEs that NDE researcher Raymond Moody has written a book called *Elvis After Life*. Some researchers believe it is only natural for people to perceive spiritual guides and heavenly beings as people they knew and admired in life.

People often claim that after they are revived their spiritual guides become like guardian angels returning to them

Christians experiencing NDEs often remember seeing Jesus as a comforting spiritual guide who returns them to life to complete unfinished tasks.

in times of stress. When she was nine years old, Sarah had an NDE in which she met a spiritual guide she called Beth. Twenty years later, Sarah claims Beth still visits her on occasion. Sarah always thought her spiritual guide was invisible to everyone but herself. When Sarah's son was going through a particularly rebellious stage—his grades in school were dropping and he was staying out late many nights—Sarah had a long conversation with her guardian angel. Sarah was unaware that her son was watching them. In the morning, he asked Sarah, "Who was that woman you were talking to last night? She seemed real nice."[47]

Life Review

NDEs can be as simple as a single out-of-body experience or can include a detailed life review. Most people feel life reviews help them learn their true purpose, changing or spiritually educating them. Often described as comprehensive and vivid, life reviews contain three-dimensional moving images that progress rapidly. A retired teacher from Long Island, New York, told NDE researcher P.M.H. Atwater that while his NDE life review happened quickly, it is easily recalled: "My whole life flashed in front of me, from that moment backwards to segments of my life. The review was not like a judgment. It was passive, more like an interesting novelty."[48]

Those who claim to have had life reviews often report a change in attitude after being revived. In 1979, Berkley Carter Mills almost died in a loading dock accident in Lynchburg, Virginia. While medical personnel worked to revive him, he claimed to have come out of his body and then was placed in front of a kind of heavenly court. At that point, a being that Mills believed to be Jesus said, "I'm going to judge you." Immediately Carter Mills's life review began with his birth. "He relived each incident in his life, including killing a mother bird when he was eight. He was so proud of that single shot until he felt the pain the bird's three babies went through when they starved to death without her."[49] The review of this incident among others caused Mills to better understand the spiritual nature of life on earth. In Atwater's book *Beyond the Light*, Carter Mills is quoted as saying, "It's not true that only humans have souls. Insects, animals, plants have souls, too."[50]

Some life reviews go beyond a person's past and into their future. As a teenager, Michele Sorensen nearly died in a skiing accident. The unconditional love and peace she found while experiencing her NDE made Sorensen reluctant to return to her body. At that point, a voice said to her, "But look what you are missing." Sorensen said she then saw "a tall blond man walking with two children. The little girl jumped up and down and her curls shook. The other was a boy. I recognized this as being my future family. I felt a longing for my husband and children even before I had met them!"[51] Sorensen returned to her body. She is now married to a former basketball player who is blond, and she has one daughter and one son.

Negative NDEs

Not all NDEs are positive or filled with love. Some are frightening. In 1955, Gloria Hipple almost died after a miscarriage. Hipple remembers being sucked headfirst down a dark black funnel. She tried grabbing the sides of the funnel, but she could not stop the force of the vacuum. Pleading for her life and her young children, she screamed, "My kids, my baby is so little. My little boy, he's only two years old!"[52] At the end of the cavity, Hipple saw a white dot. As she was drawn closer to the white dot, she realized it was actually a hideous skull with a gaping grin and blank sunken eye sockets. When she reached it, the skull shattered revealing a warm bright light as the force propelling her slowed. Soon afterward, Hipple reentered her body.

Others have been taunted by the beings they meet. In 1980, Sandra Brock succumbed to complications during surgery. Like Hipple, Brock remembers being pulled through a long, dark passageway. People from her past laughed and screamed at her. After begging to go back, Brock suddenly found herself back in her bed feeling grateful to be alive.

Some negative NDEs do not begin as a horrifying event. Nancy Evans Bush had such an experience during the premature delivery of her second child. After speeding through space, a few black and white circles appeared before her. The circles made clicking noises as they switched from black to white and back to black again. Both the clicks and the circles seemed to be mocking Bush. The message she inferred from the clicks was that life did not really exist. "The world never existed. Your family never existed. There is nothing here. There was never anything there. That's the joke—it was all a joke." The more Bush thought about her life and the world not being real, the more she grieved for it and her loved ones. "I know no one could bear that much grief, but there didn't seem to be any end to it, and no way out. Everyone I loved was gone."[53]

In her research, Atwater made several discoveries about negative or hellish NDEs. For example, if a person had difficulty coping with the trauma of dying, their NDE was more likely to be unpleasant. Interestingly, only adults seemed to experience negative NDEs. In her book *Beyond the Light*, Atwater wrote, "What I have observed in every case I have investigated is that the hellish version of near-death is a confrontation with one's shadow."[54] It would seem that negative NDEs are created by the fear of death.

A Visit to Heaven

Seeing the light and experiencing a life review often help explain life on earth. Some NDEs go further, giving the person a glimpse of heaven. Several individuals reporting visits to heaven say the beauty encountered there could not be described in words, yet it seemed more real than life on earth.

For many, the best part of heaven was uniting with their departed loved ones. A woman still mourning the death of her aunt was assured from her NDE that she would see her deceased family members again. She explained, "Best of all, our loved ones live to love and welcome us home when we are called upon to change to a higher life."[55] Several people reported being overjoyed at seeing old family pets as in this account from the book *The Eternal Journey:* "I remember distinctly of looking down upon my physical body—but my joy was complete when into my arms sprang my little dog, young and full of life."[56] In another account, a young boy was reunited with his springer spaniel and black cat. The dog licked his hand, and the cat purred at seeing the boy.

A Reluctance to Return

The love and peace that enfolds those experiencing an NDE can make it difficult to return to an earthly life. If most accounts of NDEs are real, the afterlife is paradise and death is relief from the stress of illness or the trauma of an accident. After experiencing an NDE and being resuscitated, many people initially feel depressed or angry. Some even harbor feelings of rejection, as if they were "kicked out of heaven." A subject interviewed in one of Morse's studies recalled physically resisting coming back to life while on the other side:

> I was clutching the rail because I didn't want to go back. That was the last thing I wanted to do. And the voice talked to the white light a little bit more and they decided that I would have to go back. So I threw a tantrum. I pitched a royal fit. I grabbed onto the rail of the fence and wrapped my arms and legs around it and I wouldn't let go. The voice just laughed. "Look, you can have it later, but this is not the time. And throwing a tantrum is not going to do you any good."[57]

For many, the return to life is a long, frustrating struggle in which they often begin to reexamine emotional issues they avoided for years. Geraldine Berkheimer from California explains the aftermath of the NDE in Atwater's *Beyond the Light:* "Beauty and pain go hand in hand in describing the experience. My reason for coming back, and perhaps the only reason for any of us, is to share the light which each of us is. It doesn't matter what, where, to whom, or how this is done, if it involves joy or even, on occasion, anger."[58]

Electrical Sensitivity

Once recovered from the trauma and impact of the NDE, most individuals find themselves profoundly changed. A high percentage of survivors believe they gained psychic abilities after their NDEs. Many have dreams or visions that, they claim, predict the future. An accident victim interviewed by Morse was told during an NDE that he would have a son. Before the NDE, he and his wife could not have children. The man told Morse: "A few months later we learned my wife was pregnant and our son was born almost a year to the day after my accident."[59]

Some who have survived NDEs say they are blessed with other abilities and talents. Research by both Atwater and Morse suggests a majority of near-death survivors, up to 73 percent of those surveyed, develop a condition known as electrical sensitivity. Electrical sensitivity refers to how, for unexplained reasons, some people's energy seems to affect or control electrical objects. Sometimes this sensitivity is deemed responsible for malfunctioning electronic equipment. More than half the survivors Atwater surveyed claimed televisions and computers operate strangely in their presence. For example, television pictures might become distorted and computers might freeze up or even shut down.

People with electrical sensitivity tend to be more intense emotionally, more intelligent, and are more affected by light and noise. In addition, many individuals who

A psychic healer demonstrates her abilities during a scientific experiment. Many people claim to acquire healing powers following an NDE.

developed electrical sensitivity after surviving an NDE also claim they have the ability to heal people. Some say they have cured people of various ailments simply by passing their hands over them and praying for them. Others experience miraculous recoveries themselves. When she was forty-five years old, Kathy was diagnosed with cancer of the thyroid gland. Her doctor gave her only six months to live, during which time she contracted viral pneumonia. As it became more difficult for her to breathe, Kathy succumbed to the infection. While doctors worked to save her, she felt a being of light at her side: "Yet it wasn't like a light that you see, but rather felt and understood. It touched me, and my whole body was filled with its light. It was bursting out of me. I sensed a voice telling me that my children still needed me."[60] Kathy recovered from the pneumonia. A few weeks later, to her doctor's surprise, she was also cancer free.

Changed Lives

Almost all survivors describe their NDEs as vivid, real, and memorable. These profound experiences often change people's lives. The most significant transformation near-death survivors experience is a change in attitude that precipitates new perspectives on life and new priorities. For instance, a teenager named Annie had experimented with drugs, alcohol, and sex. When she was sixteen she tried to kill herself by taking a handful of barbiturates and washing them down with vodka. She had an NDE in which her guardian angel appeared to her telling her to appreciate her life as a gift and value it. After Annie woke up in the hospital, she began to make some serious changes. "Immediately after the experience I felt as though I have been given a mission in life, like I was born to accomplish something,"[61] Annie told Melvin Morse. She stopped using drugs and alcohol and took control of her life. Today she is happily married and the mother of four sons.

Physical Explanation for NDEs

Explanations for why people experience the near-death phenomena range from overactive imaginations, the effects of drugs administered before and during resuscitation, and the strong influence of religious education. Some think that people who have NDEs are simply seeing what they want to see or what their religion has taught them to believe. Perhaps the most compelling reason to believe in NDEs is the fact that many children have had them. Some children having little or no religious training have reported NDEs similar to those of adults. However, medical research suggests NDEs are not real but hallucinations caused by the stress and trauma of pain.

Some scientists who believe NDEs are induced by trauma have discovered chemical substances in the brain that can create visions that look similar to images described by near-death survivors. In 1982, Jack Cowan, a neurobiologist at the University of Chicago, theorized that a sudden increase in excitability changes the way some fluids in the brain react. Cowan determined from his research that people whose brains are in this abnormal state would see stripes, spirals, or concentric rings that resemble the tunnels of NDEs. What Cowan's research cannot explain is why hallucinations resulting from unusual brain activity, drugs, or oxygen deprivation seem unrealistic compared to the vivid imagery of NDEs.

Perhaps the most exciting research being conducted pinpoints a location in the brain that, when stimulated, could account for out-of-body experiences. Melvin Morse and many other researchers have determined this location to be in the brain's right temporal lobe, found just above the right ear. According to Morse, "At times some patients would say 'I am leaving my body now,' when touched in this area with an electric probe. Several reported saying, 'I'm half in and half out.'"[62] This discovery, though, does not explain the light, seeing departed loved ones, or life reviews. Those experiences seem to come from outside the body. Morse believes this area of the brain is merely "the spot where the mind, body, and spirit interact."[63]

Dutch cardiologist Pim van Lommel has developed a theory that even when a brain stops working, consciousness

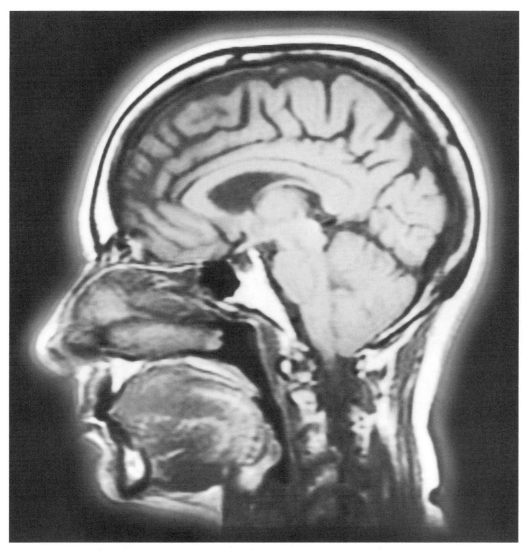

can exist. "You can compare the brain to a TV set," says van Lommel. "The TV program is not in your TV set." Van Lommel believes there is "a kind of communication between all our cells." Muscle, skeleton, gut, skin, blood, and brain cells "talk to one another in a kind of network that keeps our experience of consciousness going seamlessly even as billions of cells die and billions of others are produced." Van Lommel believes this cell communication

Some researchers believe an area of the human brain's right temporal lobe is responsible for the multitude of out-of-body experiences.

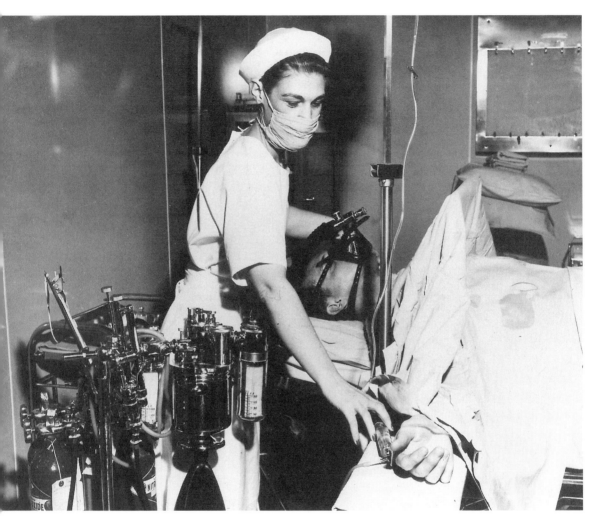

Some believe drugs administered to patients during surgery help explain why certain people experience vivid near-death phenomena.

explains the phenomena of the NDE, including why people can see life reviews and have conversations while they are technically dead.[64]

While the NDE provides some insight into what it is like to die, it does not *prove* life after death exists because no near-death survivor has actually died. However, whether NDEs are real or imagined, many more scientists and medical professionals agree the phenomenon is worth studying. Reports of this phenomenon appear to be increasing around the world. A 1992 Gallup poll listed approximately 13 million people as claiming to have had NDEs. In a Gallup survey taken ten years earlier, only 8 million people admitted to being near-death survivors. These statistics do not include children. The increased interest and the jump in the number of NDEs reported may be seen as proof that NDEs are more accepted by the medical profession, scientific community, and the general public.

Chapter 4

Communication with the Dead

Almost all major religions claim the dead survive in some form. How that belief is interpreted affects the way people all over the world grieve the loss of a loved one. But for some, belief is not enough. The need to know the fate of the departed has propelled many to seek ways to communicate with the dead. Some go to séances in hopes of contacting deceased relatives and friends, some visit places reputed to be haunted out of curiosity, and others seek visions of departed loved ones. Contacting the dead can momentarily ease grief and provide emotional support, or answer questions about the afterlife.

Ancestor Cults

Ancestor cults, believing the dead must be respected because they possess supernatural powers, can be found throughout Africa. Communication with the dead in these tribal societies is encouraged. In many of these cultures, the dead are thought to never leave their villages. Their spirits remain to watch over the living, often inhabiting the houses, fields, and cemeteries of their earthly homes. In many tribal belief systems, celebrations honor ancestors while asking the departed for help. The Pueblo Indians of the southwestern United States practice elaborate ceremonies in which people impersonate the departed and urge them to bring rain and bless their crops.

Tribal societies often use meditation and rituals to contact the dead. The African Bwiti tribe believe that by eating a medicinal plant called *iboga* and staring into a reflection from water or a mirror, a person can temporarily leave this world and visit the land of the dead. One member of the Bwiti tribe wrote a poem about his journey to meet his father on which he encountered many others seeking their ancestors:

I found myself taken by it up a long road
In a deep forest,
Until I came to a barrier of black iron.
At that barrier, unable to pass,
I saw a crowd of black persons
Also unable to pass. In the distance . . .
It was very bright.
I could see many colors in the air. . . .
Suddenly my father descended from above
In the form of a bird.
He gave me then my Eboka name
And enabled me to fly up after him
Over the barrier of iron.[65]

A nineteenth-century woodcut shows participants of a séance attempting to contact the dead.

Some believe the spirits of dead relatives take an active role in the lives of their descendants. This can include helping the living with everyday problems concerning friends, family, and work; answering questions; or foretelling the future. One way many ancient cultures connected with the dead was through the process of necromancy.

Necromancy

Necromancy is a form of magic in which a witch or sorcerer helps someone contact the dead to ask for help in living their earthly life. Both the ancient Greeks and Romans practiced necromancy. In his book *Death and the Afterlife*, Brian Innes tells the legend of a Roman leader who consulted with a witch to learn his future after growing discouraged with the confusing answers of the ancient Greek

Some cultures believe that disembodied spirits inhabit cemeteries, and that the living can commune with the dead at their gravesites.

gods, the Olympians. "Though it may be well enough for the oracles and prophets who serve the Olympians to give riddling responses, a man who dares to consult the dead deserves to be told the truth,"[66] the Roman said. The witch managed to conjure up a ghost who entered a dead body. The ghost then answered all of the Roman's questions about his future. Necromancy was so important to the Romans that even after it was outlawed for being evil, like witchcraft and sorcery, necromancy was sometimes secretly practiced.

Another account of necromancy is given in the Old Testament of the Bible. Saul, the first king of Israel, wanted to learn what would happen in an upcoming battle. After unsuccessfully relying on his dreams and consulting priests and living prophets, Saul called upon the witch of Endor to conjure up the dead prophet Samuel. In a nighttime session, the witch dug "a hole in the crust of the earth so that the world of the living may be joined to the realm of the dead." Eventually the witch tells Saul the deceased prophet has come to answer his questions. However, "only she can see the 'old man, wrapped in a robe,' and only she can actually communicate with the spirit and pass on the messages received."[67] The spirit predicted Saul will die in battle, and Saul is killed the very next day. Learning of his fate did not save Saul from it. The story of Saul warns against resorting to necromancy.

Christian doctrine condemns the conjuring of ghosts and spirits as evil. Raymond Moody, however, does not believe communicating with the dead is wrong. In fact, Moody has developed a new way to talk with departed loved ones that is based on ancient techniques.

Theater of the Mind

Theater of the Mind is a retreat established by Moody in rural Alabama where people attempt to contact specific spirits. Many ancient peoples looked into reflective pools of water or mirrors in hopes of calling forth the deceased. Moody's facility, designed to help individuals contact the dead by mirror gazing, offers several activities to help guests relax and prepare for reuniting with departed loved ones. The grounds are in a lovely natural setting where visitors can enjoy hiking. Before entering the theater, guests can visit a small art gallery. The theater itself is a series of small darkened rooms with large mirrors in them. Modern-day mirror gazers claim they have seen and sometimes talked with departed loved ones while staring into a mirror in a darkened room. The sessions are always long, lasting anywhere from ten to twenty-four hours.

According to Moody, 50 percent of the visitors to Theater of the Mind report having conversations with their visions. Some say their visions seem to appear next to them. Others say their dead relatives step out of the mirror. That was how it happened for one woman who claimed to have a reunion with her father.

> I can't say that we needed words. I just could tell what he was trying to say. We had some very personal conversations in there, about my mother mainly, but other family matters as well. It seemed like the most natural thing in the world, just like the conversations we used to have in the parlor when I was a teenager. Except now he is dead![68]

A few feel as if they are sucked into the world they envision. A twenty-six-year-old woman claimed she traveled into the mirror and met her Aunt Betty, her grandmother, and her great-grandmother: "I was so overjoyed during this whole meeting. There was not a doubt in the world they were there and that I saw them, and it was as real as meeting anyone."[69]

Unexpected Visions

Moody reported 25 percent of visitors do not see their loved ones at the facility but later after they have left the

Many ancient peoples gazed into reflective pools of water in an effort to summon forth the spirits of the dead.

grounds. "Usually such a reunion takes place within twenty-four hours,"[70] writes Moody in his book about mirror gazing, *Reunions*. One well-respected journalist went to the Alabama retreat to contact her son who had committed suicide. She had a vision of her son later in her hotel room. "I had the apparition of my son several hours after I had been in the apparition booth, and to this day I can see it as clearly as I can see the coffeepot I am looking at right now. I can see that face. If I were an artist, I could draw it."[71] The woman returned from Alabama feeling at peace, assured that her son was okay and that he loved her.

Often people do not see the relatives they expected. One elderly man came in search of his father but envisioned his two deceased cousins. When Moody himself tried to contact his maternal grandmother with whom he had a warm and loving relationship, he saw instead his paternal grandmother to whom he was not as close. Their reunion, however, helped Moody understand that relationship better. "My encounter has clarified why it is that apparition seekers do not necessarily see the person whom they have set out to see. On the basis of my own experience, I believe that the subjects see the person they need to see,"[72] writes Moody. Skeptics suggest because of the length of the mirror-gazing session and the unusual setting and atmosphere, visitors to Moody's theater are susceptible to hallucinations and it is unlikely they are truly reuniting with deceased loved ones.

Ghosts

People also claim to have seen the dead without calling upon them to appear, and sometimes these spirits are of people they have never known. Ghosts are spirits of the dead who are often associated with places where tragic events occurred. Many believe ghosts are restless spirits who died with unfinished business, which is why their souls continue to inhabit the earth. According to a 1981 Gallup poll, 11 percent of Americans and as many as 20 percent of the British believe in ghosts. Seven percent of those surveyed said they had encountered ghosts. Few of those reported they were frightened by the experience.

Some people do not see ghosts but claim to sense their presence. An Englishwoman called Viv says she feels like an intruder in her Victorian house in Northampton because it is inhabited by the spirit of an old woman who once lived there. From the day Viv moved in, odd things have happened: lights turn on and off by themselves, the central heating has switched on in the heat of summer, and household items go missing only to be found in unexpected places later. A neighbor told Viv the old woman was a recluse who collapsed and died in the kitchen. Viv believes

Ghosts are spirits typically associated with places where tragic events occurred. Some people believe that ghosts are restless spirits that died with unfinished business on earth.

the woman's spirit never left the house because the woman could not let go of her life there.

Some hauntings would be considered friendly. A Greek woman named Stella is comforted by the spirit of her dead grandmother living in her Cyprus home. Stella believes her grandmother's ghost encourages her artistic talents and tastes. For example, her grandmother's spirit often nods approval at how Stella decorated her home. Stella's claims are supported by her friend, who told Stella during one visit to her house, "I don't mean to scare you or anything but a ghost is sitting next to you."[73] Stella asked the woman what the ghost looked like, and her friend described a tall female wearing a long dress and scarf—Stella's grandmother.

Occasionally there are reports of a frightening or even evil haunting. Some believe evil spirits haunt the living instead of going on to an afterlife because they want revenge upon those who hurt them in life. In some cases, that revenge is taken upon those living where the ghosts died. Many people still believe the legendary ghost of the Bell Witch was responsible for a man's death in the early 1800s. According to various reports, the Bell family of Tennessee was tormented by the spirit of a woman buried on their farm. People believe the trouble started when John Bell angered the ghost by shooting at a stray dog which wandered onto his property. For the next two years, the Bell family and their neighbors credited the spirit of the Bell Witch with a series of unexplained and disturbing incidents. Many neighbors saw the milky image of an angry woman whose wrath was reserved for John Bell and his family. Bell's daughters felt hard slaps from an invisible hand; the Bell housekeeper was humiliated by voices screaming cruel insults at her and spitting on her; and rocks fell out of nowhere. Eventually John Bell became sick with a strange illness. Just before Christmas in 1820, Bell died. Many believed he was poisoned by the spirit of the Bell Witch.

For some people, ghosts explain strange household phenomena. Those who claim to have encountered ghosts view them as proof of life after death. Others are skeptical, believing ghosts, like other phenomena, are little more than people's active imaginations.

Dreams

Dreams have long been considered a source of inspiration, prophecy, and messages from beyond. Often people who lost a loved one dream about them. Many believe deceased relatives and friends communicate with them through their dreams to comfort them and ease their fears about death.

Carol Parrish-Harra is a minister and counselor who works with the dying and their families. She recalls the story of one of her clients who unexpectedly lost his young daughter to a short, swift illness. The man was having a difficult time getting on with his life until he dreamed about his daughter. She appeared to him in the dream, kissed him, and said, "Daddy, I love you."[74] Parrish-Harra wrote about this experience: "Within this message of love, life began again in a heart grieving and closing. She came to comfort and to heal his pain by her presence."[75] Parrish-Harra believes these dreams assure the grieving there is an afterlife and that their loved ones are safe.

A friend of Elisabeth Kübler-Ross wrote to her about a dream she had of her daughter, Katie, who died of a brain tumor. The woman described a dream in which she and her husband crossed over a stream by way of a narrow footbridge and met her daughter: "We went over to Katie and I asked if I could hold her. She said, 'Yes, we can play for a while but I cannot leave with you.' I said that I knew that. We visited and played for a while and then we had to go."[76] The woman woke that morning feeling a peace and warmth that changed her. She decided she wanted to help others, so she obtained a degree in counseling and now works with people who have AIDS.

Swiss psychiatrist Elisabeth Kübler-Ross is widely respected as an author of books that explore the nature of life after death.

Visitations from Loved Ones

Many also claim to see, hear, or feel dead relatives and friends in visions while they are awake. Visions of the departed have been commonly reported after loved ones die. Some bring unexpected information to surviving family members. One young woman named Janice claims to have seen her deceased father several weeks after his funeral. Toward the end of his life, Janice's father limped as he walked due to a bad hip. Janice awoke one morning to find her father standing next to her bed.

> I got up and walked with him to the living room. He was walking fine, without a limp. All he said was that he had tuberculosis of the bone and he wanted us to know. I don't know why it was important that we know, but when I checked with his doctor he confirmed that the bone was filled with TB.[77]

Some say this proves that Janice's father contacted her from the afterlife. Others think visions of the departed are illusions. Whether they are supernatural connections, or simply imagined to help the grieving cope, visions of deceased loved ones often bring peace and comfort to those who have them. In her book *The New Age Handbook on Death and Dying*, Parrish-Harra wrote that many people claim departed friends and relatives have appeared to them, said they loved them, and assured them not to fear the future. Parrish-Harra believes she has been visited by her dead father. She called the experience one of the most meaningful of her life. It happened one afternoon on a drive from St. Petersburg to Sarasota, Florida. She began crossing a very high bridge called the Skyway Bridge, and at the bridge's highest point, Parrish-Harra strongly felt a presence in her car: "I dared not look, but I felt my father, exactly as I had felt him so many years before when we had been together." She had felt some guilt for not visiting her father for several years before he died. Parrish-Harra asked if the presence was indeed her father. The presence answered it was. She told her father she was sorry she had not come to see him. He replied: "Everything is all right. I understand; I know." Parrish-Harra then asked to see him, "turning my head toward him, I could perceive a mist-like presence. He was heavier than when I last saw him, with less hair, but I recognized him and felt hot tears of relief and love flowing down my cheeks. I said, 'Dad, I love you,' and he reassured me, 'Don't worry, Carol. I came to you.'"[78]

Séances

Some seek the comfort, guidance, and answers they believe the dead can provide through the help of spiritual mediums and meetings known as séances. The first séance occurred in New York in the mid-1800s.

In 1848, the Fox family suspected their Hydesville, New York, home was haunted. A series of mysterious nighttime rapping noises kept John Fox, his wife, and their two youngest daughters awake for several months. The young Fox sisters claimed they could answer the raps by snapping their fingers. Mrs. Fox described how one of her daughters "talked" to these spirits: "Margaretta said, in sport, 'Now do just as I do. Count one, two, three, four,' striking one hand against the other at the same time—and the raps came as before."[79] Mrs. Fox also experimented with the strange presence in her home. She spoke directly to the spirits and asked them to tell her the ages of the Fox children by a succession of raps: "Instantly, each one of my children's ages was given correctly, pausing between them sufficiently long enough to individualize them."[80]

Eventually the Fox sisters claimed to be spiritual mediums, or people who can communicate with the spirits of the dead. The two held demonstrations of their abilities, which became known as séances. At the séance, a small group of people sat around a table while one of the Fox sisters went into a trance to allow the spirits to inhabit her body. The people asked questions that were responded to by the mysterious rappings. As mediums, the Fox sisters claimed only to provoke "spirit rappings." However, the press of the day exaggerated what went on in the Fox home, reporting that furniture seemed to rise off the floor by itself and tables mysteriously flipped over during the séances. Stories of these unusual events convinced many that the soul survives death.

The Beginning of Spiritualism

As séances like this gained in popularity throughout the second half of the nineteenth century, more people began to embrace a belief in life after death.

As the news of strange happenings in the Fox house spread, more people became interested in communication with the dead. Many of the believers in this phenomenon formed philosophical societies based on the belief in spirits and the authenticity of séances. This movement became

known as Spiritualism. Séances and Spiritualism became popular in both America and Britain. Mediums either went into trances and began speaking in the voice of a spirit or began involuntarily writing messages from the spirit world (a practice known as automatic writing).

Between 1848 and 1880, mediums began to use theatrical lighting and other illusionary effects to enhance the experience. As séances became more dramatic, so did the reports of séance happenings. In 1869, several people claimed a famous medium named D.D. Home rose out of his chair and flew out one window on the third floor and back in another during a séance. Some mediums produced photographic evidence of ghostly spirits materializing in séances and other places. Few if any would be considered authentic; most looked fake by modern standards.

Despite the fantastic and unbelievable claims of spiritual mediums and Spiritualists, many people, including several well-known individuals, embraced Spiritualism. Sir Arthur Conan Doyle, the famous novelist and creator of the detective Sherlock Holmes, was a Spiritualist. "We want to get something that will beat materialism," said Doyle referring to the philosophy that denies the existence of the soul. "We want a religion that you can prove."[81]

The belief in life after death was central to the Spiritualist philosophy, and it was comforting to many believers that mediums could provide proof of that belief. Spiritualist Gladys Osborne Leonard claimed Spiritualism gave people "back their lost faith, their hope for Eternity and reunion with those they love."[82]

For some, Spiritualism provided a glimpse into heaven. During World War II, E. Ramsden, a British squadron leader, decided to investigate claims of an afterlife. Ramsden gathered a group of grieving military families to visit a respected medium named Helen Duncan. Many of the group's deceased loved ones appeared to speak through

Sir Arthur Conan Doyle embraced Spiritualism as a way to prove the existence of the human soul.

Mrs. Duncan, assuring their relatives they were happy and free from pain and suffering. In one session, a woman from South Africa whose son died years earlier, was comforted when Duncan contacted the young man's spirit. The son told his mother how wonderful he felt about being reunited with his pet rabbit and dog in heaven. The experience convinced Ramsden there is life after death.

Messages from the Dead

The main tenet of Spiritualism is illustrated in the 1893 epitaph to Spiritualists Catharine and Levi Smith at Laurel Hill Cemetery in Philadelphia: "Life is eternal; Death is merely a change of conditions."[83] Some Spiritualists, however, wanted to provide proof of an afterlife. In 1882, several Spiritualists formed the British Society for Psychical Research (SPR) to further investigate spirit communication and life after death. The society developed several experiments hoping to prove the spirits of the dead could communicate with the living. One complicated test, called cross correspondence, involved mediums from all over the world attempting to contact different spirits, asking each for one part of a lengthy message that was decided upon while the spirits were still living. Society members claimed all parts of the message were produced, each containing quotes from classical literature concerning the subject of death. On April 16, 1907, the first part appeared when a medium named Mrs. Fleming produced a piece of automatic writing in her home in India. The message read: "Maurice, Morris. Mors. And with that the shadow of death fell upon him and his soul departed out of his limbs." The next day a London medium "spoke the words 'Sanatos, Tanatos' as she emerged from a trance. Thanatos is the Greek for 'death.'"[84] Several days later, more automatic writing generated quotations from other classical poets including Virgil and Shakespeare and finally a quotation in Latin from the Roman poet Horace.

Communicating Through Séances and Channeling

Besides cross correspondence, several SPR members promised to send messages back to their friends after they died. A message in the form of automatic writing from the

A medium and a woman use a Ouija board and a wineglass to communicate with spirits.

alleged spirit of F.W.H. Myers, one of the founders of SPR, confirms the group's belief in the afterlife and the spirits of the dead as well as the success of the cross correspondence experiment: "The nearest simile I can find to express the difficulties of sending a message is that I appear to be standing behind a sheet of frosted glass—which blurs sight and deadens sound—dictating feebly—to a reluctant and somewhat obtuse secretary."[85] Myers's spirit reportedly communicated with several of his friends after he died in 1901. One message in particular convinced Myers's friend Sir Oliver Lodge that the dead watch over the living. In 1915, Lodge attended a séance in which the spirit of Myers assured his friend that his spirit would be near him "to ease the blow which was coming."[86] The message confused Lodge until two days later when he learned his son had died in battle in France. As a convert to Spiritualism, Lodge also pledged to send a message back to the living after he died. He wrote the message then put it in a sealed envelope to be opened after his death. Despite Lodge's promise, no medium to date has reported receiving anything from the spirit of Oliver Lodge.

Although he never joined the ranks of the Spiritualists, the famous magician and escape artist Harry Houdini tried an experiment similar to Lodge's. He promised his wife that if he survived death as a spirit he would send her a series of coded messages from the other side. Houdini died on Halloween, October 31, 1926. For years after his death, Houdini's wife visited several mediums, attending a number of séances attempting to find some sign from her late husband. None came, and eventually she declared the experiment a failure. However, many modern-day Houdini fans still organize Halloween séances in hopes of communicating with the great magician's spirit.

Today's Spiritualists are most likely to consult channelers. Like mediums, channelers go into trances to summon spirits of the dead and spiritual guides to answer the questions of those attending the channeling session. Most channelers claim to have specific spiritual guides who deliver messages from the spirits of loved ones sought at channeling sessions. During channeling, the spiritual guide speaks through the channeler or the channeler begins automatic writing to convey the spirit's message.

Skeptics

Spiritualism reached its peak in popularity at the end of World War I, when people grieving the loss of husbands, brothers, and sons killed in the war went to séances to help them communicate with their loved ones. At that time, people began to seriously question the motives and

Escape artist Harry Houdini (pictured wearing a strait jacket) was a fierce critic of Spiritualism and he worked tirelessly to expose fraudulent mediums.

authenticity of spiritual mediums. Many mediums were proven to be frauds who made their living exploiting the emotions of the grieving. In 1888, the Fox sisters admitted they were frauds, saying they produced the strange rappings by cracking their toe joints.

The best-known critic of mediums and Spiritualism was Harry Houdini. Perhaps because he grieved for his mother after her death, Houdini was passionate about exposing fraudulent mediums preying upon the emotions of those in mourning. Because Houdini studied the history of magic and understood the tricks of illusion, it was relatively easy for him to reveal many mediums for what they were: frauds and highly skilled performers. In his later years, Houdini spent a great deal of his own money and a lot of time on his crusade against the charlatans of Spiritualism. One of the most respected mediums of Houdini's day was also the wife of a prominent Boston surgeon. As a medium, Mina Crandon called herself "Margery" and was very popular with the celebrities of the time. Houdini exposed Margery as a fraud through an investigation sponsored by the *Scientific American* magazine. After visiting one of Margery's séances, Houdini said he saw the woman perform a number of tricks including making noises with her feet and lifting objects which she claimed moved on their own. Houdini even went so far as to publish, at his own expense, a pamphlet outlining how the Boston medium duped her clients.

Today's Investigator

Today, Houdini is succeeded by James Randi, also known as the Amazing Randi. As a magician and escape artist, Randi has spent more than half a century investigating those involved in promoting the paranormal, occult, and supernatural. He has written several books exposing bogus psychics, astrologers, and many others who have bilked the public. In 1996, Randi founded the James Randi

Educational Foundation, a nonprofit organization dedicated to questioning and scientifically researching paranormal claims. To raise public awareness about the deceptions used to promote supernatural claims, Randi's foundation has offered a $1 million prize to "any person or persons who can demonstrate any psychic, supernatural or paranormal ability of any kind under mutually agreed upon scientific conditions."[87] While many have boasted that they can achieve this, no one has ever passed the preliminary tests to claim the foundation's prize money.

Harry Houdini exposes a favorite trick of fraudulent mediums by ringing a bell beneath a séance table with his toes.

James Randi has spent much of his life exposing bogus psychics, spiritualists, and astrologers.

Actual contact with the spirits of the dead has yet to be proved. Those who claim to have reunited with the departed provide no scientific evidence there is life after death. However, the belief in an afterlife and the spiritual survival of loved ones does bring peace and comfort to believers.

The Need to Believe

It is apparent most humans wish to survive in some form after they die. The great Indian nationalist leader Mohandas Gandhi was once quoted as saying about life after death, "We have no evidence whatsoever that the soul perishes with the body."[88] Beliefs in an afterlife are varied, but they have been with mankind since the dawn of time.

Perhaps such beliefs are so prevalent because they are useful to human societies. The idea that good people ascend to heaven and evil people are doomed to hell satisfies a sense of justice. Purgatory offers people a chance for redemption. Reincarnation ensures the opportunity to complete life's unfinished business while growing spiritually.

Talking About Death

The idea that life goes on in some form after death also comforts the dying and their families. Still it is often difficult for some to hear, understand, or accept claims of the afterlife. In his book *Life After Life*, Raymond Moody writes of how awkward it was for one man to talk about his NDE: "He can find no human words adequate to describe these unearthly episodes. He also finds that others scoff, so he stops telling other people. Still, the experience affects his life profoundly, especially his views about death and its relationship to life."[89]

Indian leader Mohandas Gandhi believed that the human soul did not die with its earthly body. For many, this belief gives meaning to life itself.

Kübler-Ross describes a similar case of a twelve-year-old girl who was afraid to tell her mother about her NDE. "I don't want to tell my mommy that there is a nicer home than ours,"[90] she told Kübler-Ross. Eventually she told her father and included details about meeting her brother in heaven. Her father believed her then because the girl never knew she had a brother, who died a few months before his sister was born. Talking about their NDEs has proved to help both near-death survivors and their families cope with such a profound and emotionally challenging event.

Comforting Evidence

The increasing number of reported NDEs, psychic visions of departed loved ones, and other glimpses into what lies beyond death make it difficult to completely dismiss the idea of an afterlife. While such experiences can rarely be measured by scientific methods, many believe researching such phenomena will provide answers to questions about life on Earth. Melvin Morse believes understanding death and the dying process helps people put aside their fears and better cope with their grief. Morse wrote, "I believe that a better understanding of the dying process and a willingness to accept the spiritual visions of the dying . . . help lessen our fear of death. And by that I mean the fear the doctors feel as well as the dying patients."[91] Similarly, in her book *The Case for Heaven*, Mally Cox-Chapman wrote about a three-year-old girl named Midgie who succumbed to a degenerative disease. Midgie told her mother about an NDE: "I've been to play in God's garden, Mummy," said Midgie. "It was so, so beautiful there. He said I could come back to play tomorrow. You won't mind, will you, Mummy?"[92] The next day Midgie died. Throughout her life, Midgie's mother was comforted by her daughter's account of God's garden.

Carl Jung thought the belief in an afterlife was essential for humans to be comforted when confronted with their own or a loved one's mortality. According to Jung, if one believes in spiritual eternity, death can be thought of as joyful and a time for their soul to find enlightenment. For many, the promise of an afterlife gives meaning to life itself.

Notes

Introduction: After We Die

1. William Aldis Wright, ed., *The Complete Works of William Shakespeare: The Cambridge Edition Text.* Philadelphia: Blakiston, 1936, p. 752.
2. Elisabeth Kübler-Ross, *The Wheel of Life: A Memory of Living and Dying.* New York: Scribner's, 1997, p. 7.
3. George Gallup Jr., *Adventures in Immortality: A Look Beyond the Threshold of Death.* New York: McGraw-Hill, 1982, p. 1.

Chapter 1: Where Do People Go After They Die?

4. Ake Hultkrantz, *The Religions of American Indians.* Berkeley: University of California Press, 1979, p. 129.
5. Jal Dastur Cursetji Pavry, *The Zoroastrian Doctrine of a Future Life.* New York: Columbia University Press, 1926, pp. 92–93.
6. The Bible, Job 14:11 King James Version.
7. The Bible, Daniel 12:2 King James.
8. The Bible, I Corinthians 2:9 King James.
9. Quoted in Richard Cavendish, *Visions of Heaven and Hell.* New York: Harmony, 1977, p. 86.
10. John Ashton and Tom Whyte, *The Quest for Paradise: Visions of Heaven and Eternity in the World's Myths and Religions.* San Francisco: HarperCollins, 2001, p. 82.
11. Betty J. Eadie, *Embraced by the Light: The Most Profound and Complete Near-Death Experience Ever.* New York: Bantam, 1994, p. 78.
12. Quoted in Craig R. Lundahl and Harold A. Widdison, *The Eternal Journey: How Near-Death Experiences Illuminate Our Earthly Lives.* New York: Warner, 1997, p. 172.
13. Quoted in Ashton and Whyte, *The Quest for Paradise*, p. 76.
14. Geddes MacGregor, *Images of Afterlife: Beliefs from Antiquity to Modern Times.* New York: Paragon House, 1992, p. 173.
15. Quoted in Cavendish, *Visions of Heaven and Hell*, p. 106.
16. Quoted in Cavendish, *Visions of Heaven and Hell*, p. 106.
17. Quoted in James A. Lewis, *The Death and Afterlife Book: The Encyclopedia of Death, Near Death and Life After Death.* Detroit: Visible Ink, 2001, p. 295.
18. Quoted in Colleen McDannell and Bernhard Lang, *Heaven: A History.* New Haven, CT: Yale University Press, 2001, p. 85.

Chapter 2: Reincarnation

19. Quoted in Brian Innes, *Death and the Afterlife.* New York: St. Martin's, 1999, p. 124.

20. Quoted in Rimpoche Nawang Gehlek, *Good Life, Good Death: Tibetan Wisdom on Reincarnation.* New York: Riverhead, 2001, p. ix.
21. Quoted in Carol Bowman, *Return to Heaven: Beloved Relatives Reincarnated Within Your Family.* New York: HarperCollins, 2001, p. 122.
22. Gehlek, *Good Life, Good Death*, p. 19.
23. Quoted in Lewis, *The Death and Afterlife Book*, p. 185.
24. MacGregor, *Images of Afterlife*, p. 91.
25. Quoted in Paul Edwards, *Reincarnation: A Critical Examination.* New York: Prometheus, 1996, p. 52.
26. Quoted in Edwards, *Reincarnation*, p. 53.
27. Brian Weiss, *Many Lives, Many Masters: The True Story of a Prominent Psychiatrist, His Young Patient, and the Past-Life Therapy That Changed Both Their Lives.* New York: Simon and Schuster, 1988, p. 10.
28. Jenny Cockell, *Across Time and Death: A Mother's Search for Her Past Life Children.* New York: Simon and Schuster, 1993, p. vi.
29. Quoted in Bowman, *Return to Heaven*, p. 162.
30. Quoted in Edwards, *Reincarnation*, p. 55.
31. Tom Shroder, *"Old Souls: The Scientific Evidence for Past Lives.* New York: Simon and Schuster, 1993, p. 19.
32. Quoted in Shroder, *Old Souls*, p. 24.
33. Quoted in David Darling, *Soul Search: Scientist Explores the Afterlife.* New York: Villard, 1995, p. xxii.

Chapter 3: Near-Death Experiences
34. Quoted in P.M.H. Atwater, *Beyond the Light: What Isn't Being Said About Near Death Experiences.* New York: Carol, 1994, p. 22.
35. Atwater, *Beyond the Light*, p. 22.
36. Quoted in Raymond Moody, *Life After Life.* New York: Bantam 1986, p. 35.
37. Quoted in Moody, *Life After Life*, p. 26.
38. Quoted in Moody, *Life After Life*, p. 31.
39. Quoted in Moody, *Life After Life*, p. 32.
40. Melvin Morse and Paul Perry, *Closer to the Light: Learning from the Near-Death Experiences of Children.* New York: Ivy, 1990, p. 132.
41. Quoted in Atwater, *Beyond the Light*, p. 59.
42. Quoted in Morse and Perry, *Closer to the Light*, p. 132.
43. Quoted in Morse and Perry, *Closer to the Light*, p. 72.
44. Quoted in Morse and Perry, *Closer to the Light*, p. 145.
45. Quoted in Morse and Perry, *Closer to the Light*, p. 149.
46. Quoted in Melvin Morse and Paul Perry, *Transformed by the Light: Powerful Effects of Near-Death Experiences on People's Lives.* New York: Villard, 1992, p. 23.
47. Quoted in Morse and Perry, *Closer to the Light*, p. 152.
48. Quoted in Atwater, *Beyond the Light*, p. 16.
49. Quoted in Atwater, *Beyond the Light*, p. 67.
50. Quoted in Atwater, *Beyond the Light*, p. 67.

51. Quoted in Morse and Perry, *Closer to the Light*, p. 140.
52. Quoted in Atwater, *Beyond the Light*, p. 30.
53. Quoted in Atwater, *Beyond the Light*, p. 44.
54. Atwater, *Beyond the Light*, p. 45.
55. Quoted in Lundahl and Widdison, *The Eternal Journey*, p. 175.
56. Quoted in Lundahl and Widdison, *The Eternal Journey*, p. 143.
57. Quoted in Morse and Perry, *Transformed by the Light*, p. 53.
58. Quoted in Atwater, *Beyond the Light*, p. 124.
59. Quoted in Morse and Perry, *Transformed by the Light*, p. 115.
60. Quoted in Morse and Perry, *Transformed by the Light*, p. 142.
61. Quoted in Morse and Perry, *Transformed by the Light*, p. 153.
62. Morse and Perry, *Closer to the Light*, p. 118.
63. Morse and Perry, *Transformed by the Light*, p. 195.
64. Quoted in Anita Bartholomew, "After Life: The Scientific Case for the Human Soul," *Reader's Digest*, August 2003, p. 127.

Chapter 4: Communication with the Dead

65. Quoted in Raymond Moody and Paul Perry, *Reunions: Visionary Encounters with Departed Loved Ones*. New York: Villard, 1993, p. 69.
66. Quoted in Innes, *Death and the Afterlife*, p. 116.
67. Quoted in McDannell and Lang, *Heaven*, p. 6.
68. Quoted in Moody and Perry, *Reunions*, pp. 130–31.
69. Quoted in Moody and Perry, *Reunions*, p. 123.
70. Moody and Perry, *Reunions*, p. 119.
71. Quoted in Moody and Perry, *Reunions*, p. 119.
72. Moody and Perry, *Reunions*, p. 29.
73. Quoted in Natalie Osborne-Thomason, *The Ghost Hunting Casebook*. London: Blandford, 1999, p. 53.
74. Quoted in Carol Parrish-Harra, *The New Age Handbook on Death and Dying*. Santa Monica, CA: IBS, 1982, p. 71.
75. Parrish-Harra, *The New Age Handbook on Death and Dying*, p. 71.
76. Quoted in Kübler-Ross, *The Wheel of Life*, p. 266.
77. Quoted in Morse and Perry, *Transformed by the Light*, p. 168.
78. Parrish-Harra, *The New Age Handbook on Death and Dying*, p. 125.
79. Quoted in Innes, *Death and the Afterlife*, p. 118.
80. Quoted in Innes, *Death and the Afterlife*, p. 119.
81. Quoted in McDannell and Lang, *Heaven*, p. 294.
82. Quoted in McDannell and Lang, *Heaven*, p. 294.
83. Quoted in McDannell and Lang, *Heaven*, p. 294.
84. Quoted in Innes, *Death and the Afterlife*, p. 123.
85. Quoted in Innes, *Death and the Afterlife*, p. 123.

86. Quoted in Troy Taylor, *The Ghost Hunters Guidebook: The Essential Guide to Investigating Ghosts and Hauntings.* Alton, IL: Whitechapel, 1999, p. 35.

87. James Randi Foundation. www.randi.org.

Epilogue: The Need to Believe

88. Quoted in Mally Cox-Chapman, *The Case for Heaven: Near-Death Experiences as Evidence of the Afterlife.* New York: G.P. Putnam Sons, 1995, p. 1.

89. Moody, *Life After Life*, p. 23.

90. Quoted in Kübler-Ross, *The Wheel of Life*, p. 175.

91. Morse and Perry, *Transformed by the Light*, p. 203.

92. Quoted in Cox-Chapman, *The Case for Heaven*, p. 191.

For Further Reading

Books

Carol Bowman, *Children's Past Lives: How Past Life Memories Affect Your Child.* New York: Bantam, 1998. An interesting collection of children's past-life memories.

Ruth Brandon, *The Life and Many Deaths of Harry Houdini.* New York: Kodansha International, 1995. Excellent biography of the great magician and escape artist that includes his questions about the afterlife and the possiblity of contacting the dead.

Raymond Moody, *The Light Beyond.* New York: Bantam, 1988. A sequel to the groundbreaking *Life After Life*, including new case studies and new research on NDEs.

Kenneth Ring and Evelyn Elsaesser Valarino, *Lessons from the Light: What We Can Learn from the Near-Death Experience.* Portsmouth, NH: Moment Point, 2000. Case studies and analysis by one of the world's best-known near-death researchers.

Carol Zaleski, *Otherworld Journeys: Accounts of Near-Death Experience in Medieval and Modern Times.* New York: Oxford University Press, 1987. Written by a professor of religious studies, this book looks at the medieval visions of saints and martyrs and compares them with modern accounts of NDEs.

Websites

International Association of Near-Death Studies (www.iands.org). Has current research on NDEs and information about the phenomena.

James Randi Educational Foundation (www. randi.org). Includes details about the foundation's educational programs and some of its latest research into paranormal phenomena.

Works Consulted

Books

John Ashton and Tom Whyte, *The Quest for Paradise: Visions of Heaven and Eternity in the World's Myths and Religions.* San Francisco: HarperCollins, 2001. Beautifully illustrated volume covering many different world cultures and views about a heavenly afterlife.

P.M.H. Atwater, *Beyond the Light: What Isn't Being Said About Near Death Experiences.* New York: Carol, 1994. A comprehensive look at NDEs by a woman who had three such experiences herself and has devoted much of her life to researching the subject.

Carol Bowman, *Return to Heaven: Beloved Relatives Reincarnated Within Your Family.* New York: HarperCollins, 2001. Accounts of children recalling past lives with their present relatives.

Richard Cavendish, *Visions of Heaven and Hell.* New York: Harmony, 1977. A thorough examination of different concepts of heaven and hell.

Jenny Cockell, *Across Time and Death: A Mother's Search for Her Past Life Children.* New York: Simon and Schuster, 1993. An interesting first-person account of a woman who believes she left many children behind after dying in a past life. She writes in detail about her detective work in finding out who she had been and where her children now are.

Harold Coward, ed., *Life After Death in World Religions.* Maryknoll, NY: Orbis, 2001. A collection of essays on religious beliefs concerning the afterlife.

Mally Cox-Chapman, *The Case for Heaven: Near-Death Experiences as Evidence of the Afterlife.* New York: G.P. Putnam Sons, 1995. Written from a generally Christian perspective, this book gives several accounts of NDEs and how they affected survivors and their families.

David Darling, *Soul Search: A Scientist Explores the Afterlife.* New York: Villard, 1995. Well-written volume investigating scientific research concerning the existence of the afterlife.

Betty J. Eadie, *Embraced by the Light: The Most Profound and Complete Near-Death Experience Ever.* New York: Bantam, 1994. A very personal account of one woman's positive NDE.

Paul Edwards, *Reincarnation: A Critical Examination.* New York: Prometheus,

1996. Well-researched book claiming there is little or no evidence that reincarnation is real.

Mircea Eliade, *From Primitives to Zen*. San Francisco: Harper & Row, 1978. Contains descriptions of ancestor worship in Central Africa.

George Gallup Jr., *Adventures in Immortality: A Look Beyond the Threshold of Death*. New York: McGraw-Hill, 1982. The comprehensive report on the famous pollster's survey on death, NDEs, and views about the afterlife.

Rimpoche Nawang Gehlek, *Good Life, Good Death: Tibetan Wisdom on Reincarnation*. New York: Riverhead, 2001. The author, a former Tibetan lama, describes and explains the Tibetan Buddhist views on reincarnation.

Ake Hultkrantz, *The Religions of American Indians*. Berkeley: University of California Press, 1979. Well-documented and researched volume on religions of Native Americans from North, Central, and South America.

Brian Innes, *Death and the Afterlife*. New York: St. Martin's, 1999. Well-illustrated, fairly comprehensive discussion of various afterlife beliefs.

Elisabeth Kübler-Ross, *The Wheel of Life: A Memory of Living and Dying*. New York: Scribner's, 1997. A very personal account of the well-known psychiatrist's experiences with channeling, reincarnation, and NDEs.

James A. Lewis, *The Death and Afterlife Book: The Encyclopedia of Death, Near Death and Life After Death*. Detroit: Visible Ink, 2001. A comprehensive listing of paranormal phenomena including basic explanations.

Craig R. Lundahl and Harold A. Widdison, *The Eternal Journey: How Near-Death Experiences Illuminate Our Earthly Lives*. New York: Warner, 1997. A well-researched and varied account of NDEs and similar experiences.

Geddes MacGregor, *Images of Afterlife: Beliefs from Antiquity to Modern Times*. New York: Paragon House, 1992. Explains the basic views held by the world's major religions.

Vicki MacKenzie, *Reincarnation: The Boy Lama*. Boston: Wisdom, 1988. A biography of one young Spanish boy who is believed to be the reincarnation of a Tibetan lama.

Colleen McDannell and Bernhard Lang, *Heaven: A History*. New Haven, CT: Yale University Press, 2001. Descriptions and beliefs about heaven from ancient times to the present are thoroughly discussed.

Raymond Moody, *Life After Life*. New York: Bantam, 1986. One of the first and best-known books about research into NDEs.

Raymond Moody and Paul Perry, *Reunions: Visionary Encounters with Departed Loved Ones.* New York: Villard, 1993. Describes Moody's research into modern-day mirror gazing.

Melvin Morse and Paul Perry, *Closer to the Light: Learning from the Near-Death Experiences of Children.* New York: Ivy, 1990. Research collected for Morse's study of children who had NDEs.

———, *Transformed by the Light: Powerful Effects of Near Death Experiences on People's Lives.* New York: Villard, 1992. Morse continues his research to include the effects of NDEs on both adults and children.

Natalie Osborne-Thomason, *The Ghost Hunting Casebook.* London: Blandford, 1999. Case studies of several different kinds of ghost sightings including famous cases like the Bell Witch ghost.

Carol Parrish-Harra, *The New Age Handbook on Death and Dying.* Santa Monica, CA: IBS, 1982. Written by a grief counselor, this book helps the dying and their families cope with their experiences.

Jal Dastur Cursetji Pavry, *The Zoroastrian Doctrine of a Future Life.* New York: Columbia University Press, 1926. Offers a detailed explanation of the Zoroastrian journey to the afterlife.

Maurice Rawlings, *Beyond Death's Door.* New York: Bantam, 1979. Written by a cardiologist who has resuscitated many people claiming to have had NDEs, this book claims that many people have negative NDEs but do not remember them. Rawlings's study has been questioned by other NDE researchers.

Tom Shroder, *Old Souls: The Scientific Evidence for Past Lives.* New York: Simon and Schuster, 1993. Journalist Shroder offers a well-written account of past-life researcher Ian Stevenson as he travels the globe interviewing adults and children who remember and are affected by alleged past lives.

Ninian Smaart and Richard D. Hecht, eds., *Sacred Texts of the World: A Universal Anthology.* New York: Crossroad, 1982. Includes a poem of African tribesman giving honor to his ancestors.

Troy Taylor, *The Ghost Hunters Guidebook: The Essential Guide to Investigating Ghosts and Hauntings.* Alton, IL: Whitechapel, 1999. Describes how hauntings and other paranormal phenomena are investigated.

Brian Weiss, *Many Lives, Many Masters: The True Story of a Prominent Psychiatrist, His Young Patient, and the Past-Life Therapy That Changed Both Their Lives.* New York: Simon and Schuster, 1988. The book is considered a classic to many researching evidence of reincarnation and past lives.

William Aldis Wright, ed., *The Complete Works of William Shakespeare: The*

Cambridge Edition Text. Philadelphia: Blakiston, 1936. A collection of William Shakespeare's writings.

Periodical

Anita Bartholomew, "After Life: The Scientific Case for the Human Soul," *Readers Digest*, August 2003.

Internet Sources

The James Randi Educational Foundation. www.randi.org

Kevin Williams, "NDEs of the Rich and Famous: Hollywood Sees the Light." Near Death Experiences and the Afterlife, 2003. www.near-death.com.

Index

Picture Credits

About the Author

Nancy Hoffman has written several books including *Fairies* (also part of Lucent's Mystery Library), *Heart Transplants* (part of Lucent's Great Medical Discovery series), *West Virginia, South Carolina,* and *Eleanor Roosevelt and the Arthurdale Experiment.* She lives in Nashville, Tennessee, with her husband, Tony, and daughters, Eva and Chloe.